Every recipe in this book gives information on:

– the **number** of servings
– the **preparation time**, including cooking time
– the **nutritional value** per portion

The following symbols are used:

■ = simple
■■ = more complicated
■■■ = demanding

Kcal = kilocalories (1 Kcal = 4.184 kJ)
P = protein
F = fat
C = carbohydrate

NB   1g protein contains about 4 Kcal
      1g fat contains about 9 Kcal
      1g carbohydrate contains about 4 Kcal

tbsp = tablespoon (15ml)
tsp = teaspoon (5ml)

All temperatures are given in Fahrenheit and refer to the settings used on conventional electric ovens.

– If you have a fan-assisted oven, the temperatures given should be reduced by 85°F.
– Times and settings for microwave ovens are given only in the section on Microwave Recipes.

CREATIVE MEAT DISHES

RECIPES AND PHOTOGRAPHY

AN INTRODUCTION TO MEAT

– Friedrich W. Ehlert –
– Odette Teubner, Kerstin Mosny –

HEARTY HOME COOKING

– Rotraud Degner –
– Pete Eising –

DISHES FROM AROUND THE WORLD

– Rotraud Degner –
– Ulrich Kerth –

COOKING FOR SPECIAL OCCASIONS

– Marianne Kaltenbach –
– Rolf Feuz –

WHOLEFOOD RECIPES

– Doris Katharina Hessler –
– Ansgar Pudenz –

QUICK-AND-EASY RECIPES

– Cornelia Adam –
– Michael Brauner –

MICROWAVE RECIPES

– Monika Kellermann –
– Odette Teubner, Kerstin Mosny –

LEAN CUISINE

– Monika Kellermann –
– Anschlag & Goldmann –

Translated by UPS Translations, London
Edited by Josephine Bacon and Ros Cocks

CLB 4214
Published originally under the title
"Das Neue Menu: Fleisch"
by Mosaik Verlag GmbH, Munich
© Mosaik Verlag, Munich
Project co-ordinator: Peter Schmoeckel
Editors: Ulla Jacobs, Cornelia Klaeger, Heidrun Schaaf, Dr Renate Zeltner
Layout: Peter Pleischl, Paul Wollweber
English translation copyright © 1995 by CLB Publishing, Godalming, Surrey, UK

The JG Press imprint is a trademark of JG Press, Inc.
455 Somerset Avenue
North Dighton, MA 02764

CREATIVE
MEAT DISHES

JG PRESS

Contents

Introduction to Meat

Despite a number of health scares, beef, veal, pork, and lamb are as popular as ever. There is really no reason for anyone to exclude them from their diet, as good quality meat, eaten in moderation, plays an important part in satisfying the body's needs. Although meat contains valuable protein, essential vitamins, and minerals, it is not essential to eat it every day. How can you tell good quality meat, how do you cook it and – last but not least – which cut is best suited for which dish? The following introduction will provide all the information you need.

BEEF

Beef comes from oxen, heifers, bullocks, cows, and bulls. The quality depends on the sex and age of the animal, the type of feed, and how well it has been reared. How a carcass is hung, the maturation process of the meat, and the stresses suffered by the animal before slaughter are other important factors.

Cuts that are low in connective tissue (gristle), such as sirloin and filet, are used mainly for frying and broiling and should always be well hung. While meat is hanging, lactic acid forms within the fibers and this helps to break down any connective tissue. In this way beef becomes more tender, more digestible, and retains its flavor. Other cuts are also improved by hanging.

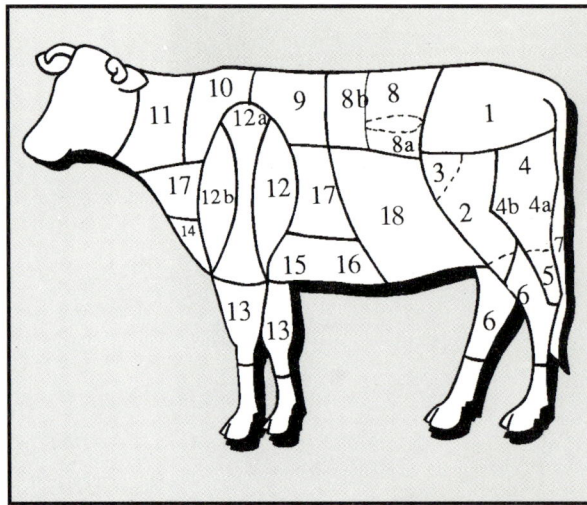

4a. Rolled topside
Steaks are cut from the rolled topside of young fattened beasts and are suitable for roasting, marinating, and broiling.

4b. Top round
This tender cut of beef can be sliced into steaks, but may also be boiled or casseroled. It is usually cooked in broth.

CUTS

Sirloin, filet, and tenderloin are the best cuts of beef, but many others provide very satisfying dishes, given the right cooking methods. Cuts that are low in connective tissue are not suited to boiling and braising, while a joint that is high in connective tissue is not suitable for roasting or frying, but is better boiled or braised. For tender, appetizing meat, the tougher tissues need moisture while cooking.

HALLMARKS OF QUALITY

Generally, beef should be deep red in color, give off a pleasant smell and display a fine-grained, marbled texture. Fresh beef should feel firm when handled. When cut, the flesh should glisten at the point of incision. If the surface of the cut is pressed lightly for a few seconds, no imprint should remain.

The beef in stores and supermarkets is generally from animals less than two years old. Meat from older animals is usually used in the production of sausages and other processed meats.

1. Round
This cut is tender, succulent and relatively low in connective tissue. Round eye can be fried, but the rump is also suitable for roasting and braising.

3. Plate
This cut is found inside the flank and may be used in goulash, stews, and other braised beef dishes.

5. Top or tip
A relatively tender cut with hardly any fatty tissue, top or tip is ideal in steak tartare and beef olives, but can also be roasted.

2. Hip, sirlion
Low in fat and connective tissue (gristle), this cut is ideal for beef olives or steak tartare.

4. Flank, shin
These hindquarters consist of shin, round, topside, and flank.

6. Leg
The thigh and shin yields good meat for soups and broths.

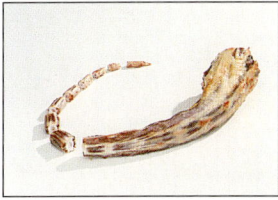

7. Oxtail
Oxtail flesh is firm and gelatinous. The thicker end of the tail is best stewed, while the thinner end is used in soups.

9. Short loin
Flesh from the fore rib is generally stewed or boiled, but it can also be broiled and roasted.

12a. Bladebone
This cut may be boiled or used in braised beef dishes. The layer of fat should be removed before cooking.

15. Brisket
Available fresh or salted, brisket should be boiled or stewed.

8. Sirloin
Sirloin steaks include rump, minute, and T-bone (1½-2½ inches thick, 1 pound 6 ounces - 2 pounds).

10. Back rib
The succulent flesh is ideal for frying and for making stews.

12b. Thick rib
This cut resembles filet in appearance, although the flesh is tougher. It is often used in thick soups, larded roasts and stews.

16. Middle brisket
This part of the breast has fewer bones and is leaner than other breast cuts. The flesh is often used in soups.

8a. Filet
Filet of beef can be roasted whole or cut into portions. Steaks are cut from the thick end, while the middle is used for *Châteaubriand* or Porterhouse.

11. Neck
This cut may be stewed, boiled or roasted. The ground meat is often added to soups.

13. Shin
The meat from the lower leg is perfect for soups, but butchers often sell shin cut into slices with the marrowbone.

17. Spareribs
The animal's rib cage provides meat for stewing. The rib bones can be cut away from the boiled flesh.

8b. Rib
Butchers prepare cutlets, rib steaks, double rib steaks and jroasts from this part of the sirloin.

12. Leg-of-mutton cut
This superb cut of beef can be boiled or used in beef olives and braised beef dishes.

14. Clod
Sold with the breast bones, clod is usually available untrimmed. It is suitable for boiling.

18. Flank
With bones or rolled without bones, flank is suitable for boiling and stewing.

1. Round
Round is the most tender but also the most expensive cut from the top of the calf's leg and can be used as steaks, cutlets, and scallops *(scaloppini)*.

2. Topside
This part of the leg is not quite so tender as the round and is best served braised.

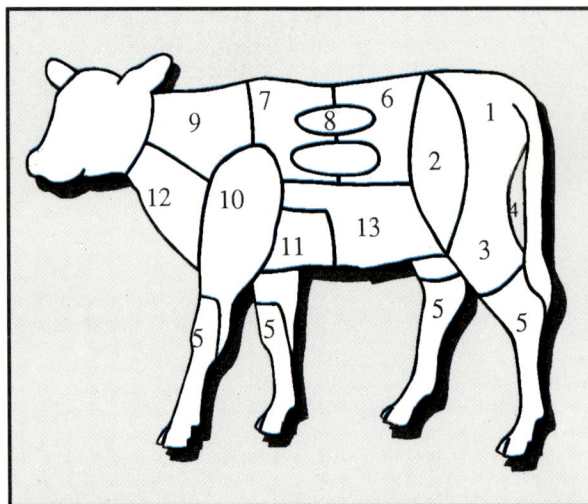

VEAL CUTS

Veal is a tender and easily digestible meat with a fine-fibered structure and no distinctive smell. Even the meat from fattened calves is low in fat and is usually covered by only a thin layer of white, fatty tissue.

Favorite cuts are leg and loin. Round, topside, thick flank, and silverside from the leg provide veal scallops. Veal is white to light pink and can be broiled, fried, stewed, or braised.

10. Shoulder
Of comparable quality to the meat from the leg, shoulder can be roasted, boiled, braised, cut into steaks, or strips, or rolled.

11. Breast
A juicy, tasty meat which is often stuffed and roasted, but tastes just as good boiled, braised, or rolled.

3. Thick flank
The thick flank provides excellent meat for steaks and scallops. Use this joint for the classic Wiener Schnitzel.

5. Knuckle
Covered by sinewy tissues, the knuckle can be roasted whole or cut into slices.

8. Filet
Veal medallions, the most tender and most popular veal cuts, are cut from the filet, but this cut can also be roasted whole.

12. Rack
If the fatty tissue and bones are removed, scrag makes a lean cut which can be boiled or braised. Rack is also served like rack of lamb.

4. Silverside
The fibers on this cut are tougher than on the thick flank and make good veal olives or a larded roast.

6.,7. Loin
Loin consists of two smaller cuts, (6) loin chops and (7) cutlets. The filet and kidneys can be found underneath.

9. Neck
Although tasty and succulent, the meat contains bones, tissue and sinews.

13. Flank
Moist cooking is essential to make this thin cut tender.

PORK

Despite some concern over its possible health risks, pork remains very popular. This is because pork is economical, has a strong, succulent flavor and is usually the main constituent in sausages.

HALLMARKS OF QUALITY

The quality of pork has been the source of some discussion. One reason is that meat from factory-farmed pigs tends to shrink when fried, becoming tough and dry. For many years, pig farmers have tried to please consumers, who tend to prefer less fat. It is certainly true that when reared in this way pigs are meatier, but the quality is much poorer.

Good quality pork should be permeated by fine streaks of fat, so that it stays tender and succulent when cooked. A thin layer of fat prevents the meat losing its juices and flavor. Surfaces should be moist and gleaming when cut. Unlike beef, pork does not need to be hung.

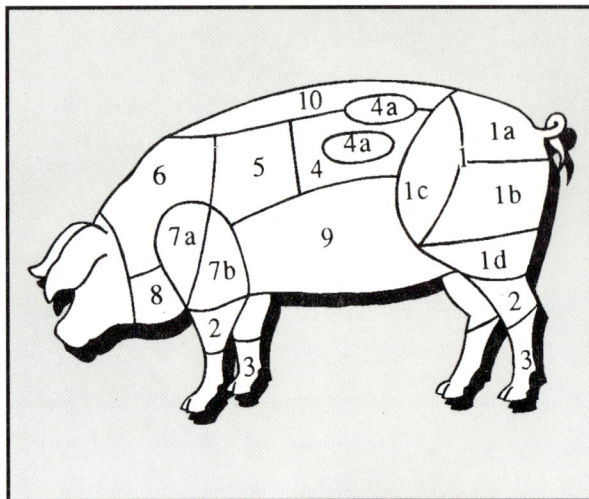

CUTS

There are numerous ways of cooking cuts of pork. Fried or broiled chops or steaks are favorites for quick and simple dishes, but pork can just as easily be used in special recipes, such as peppered pork or glazed spare ribs. The addition of ground pork to a meatloaf creates a really juicy dish.

1. Leg
The leg is the firmest and meatiest part of the pig. The flesh is covered with a thin layer of fat which adds to the taste. Whether fresh, cured, smoked, roasted, or boiled, leg of pork retains its flavor.

The various raw and cooked meats derived from pork are usually made from the leg or thigh. The characteristic flavors of different types of hams vary from region to region, depending on the methods used for curing or smoking.

If a ham is cooked whole, the rind should be scored in a diamond pattern, so that the layer of fat immediately underneath can drain away.

1a. Fillet end
This is the most tender part of the leg and is almost as good as filet. It is suitable for frying as a scallop or a steak or roasting whole.

1b. Shank end
Most pork scallops are cut across the fibers of this joint, but the tender meat from the middle leg can also be roasted whole. Cooked or smoked rolled hams are prepared from this section.

1c. Butt end
Most boiled hams come from this cut. Although many tendons permeate the flesh, it still fries well. Round end may also be roasted or boiled whole. Butchers will supply round end cured or uncured.

1d. Shoulder

Usually sold as a cut for roasting or rolled with or without rind, the shoulder is a good choice for rolled roasts and scallops. It is also used for cooked and smoked hams.

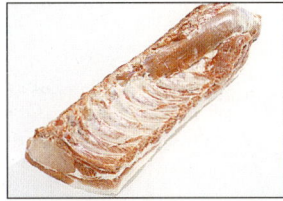

4.,5.,6. Loin

Loin of pork consists of three sections, the saddle, i.e. the part with the short ribs, filets and kidneys, rack of pork and the neck. The saddle and chops are sometimes known as the carré.

5. Rack of pork

Pork chops are usually cut from this joint, but it is sometimes cured whole, either raw or cooked, and then sold as smoked ribs. When combined with the saddle, it is used for smoked rib of pork.

8. Breast

Pork breast is sold fresh or cured and can be roasted or boiled. Stuffed pork breast, ribs, goulash, and various thick soups are some of the dishes prepared from this cut.

2. Knuckle

This is usually described as fore or hind knuckle. Whether fresh or cured, knuckle can be boiled or roasted. It is another cut which is prepared differently in various countries and regions.

4. Mid-loin

Mid-loin may be boiled, roasted, broiled, glazed or baked in pastry.

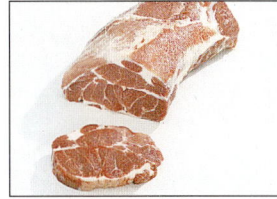

6. Boston shoulder

This succulent cut streaked with fat and connective tissue is ideal for casseroles, roasts, goulash, ragoûts and pork strips. Spare ribs can be cooked whole or broiled in portions.

9. Belly

Sold fresh or cured, with or without bones, belly of pork can be stuffed, roasted or boiled, served warm or cold in aspic. Bacon is made from the cured belly or the joint and is sold smoked or unsmoked.

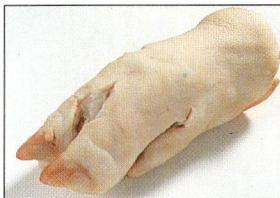

3. Feet

Pig's feet are available fresh or cured and can be boiled, roasted, broiled or stuffed. They are sometimes used to enhance thick soups, sauces, and broths. In France pig's feet are served with truffles.

4a. Filet (tenderloin)

Like most other types of meat, filet of pork is the tenderest, juiciest and leanest meat. This fine cut is often roasted whole or in a crisp coating, such as puff pastry. It can also be prepared with vegetables or in a pork caul.

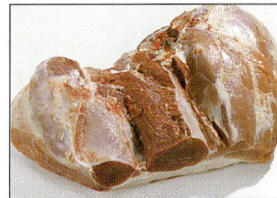

7a., 7b. Shoulder

The flesh from the shoulder is sold untrimmed with bones and rind and can be used for shoulder ham, stews, goulash, blanquette, peppered pork, and fricassées. Lean meat can be used to make ground pork.

10. Back fat

Back fat is used for barding, larding and in pâtés.
It is available from many good-quality butchers salted, unsalted, and smoked.

1. Leg of lamb

Cooked whole with or without bones, leg of lamb can be boiled, roasted, broiled, and even occasionally cured. A large leg of lamb can be halved by cutting along the bone.

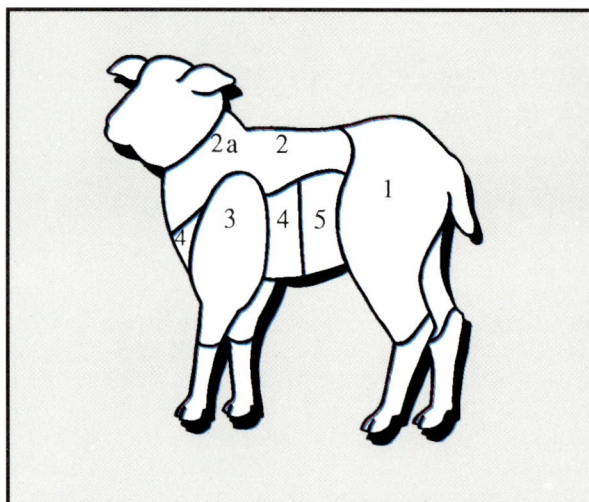

3. Shoulder of lamb

The meat from the shoulder is particularly tender and suitable not just for braising, but also for roasting and boiling. Shoulder cuts are sold whole, rolled, or cubed.

2. Loin of lamb

Loin of lamb consists of saddle, chop and best end of neck. The filets and kidneys are found beneath the loin. The whole cut is sold untrimmed or halved lengthways to make loin chops, cutlets and medallions.

LAMB

Milk-fed lamb, fattened lamb, and spring lamb are the commonest types of lamb sold. Lamb is reared in the U.S. and imported from New Zealand. Lamb is becoming more popular and more available in the U.S. It is now being reared extensively in Texas.

HALLMARKS OF QUALITY

Young lamb ranges from the light, white meat of the milk-fed lamb (up to 6 weeks old) to the pink flesh of the fattened lamb (up to 12 months). Mutton, from older sheep, is dark red and coarse-fiberd, but is no longer popular.

Well-hung lamb is deep red in color and should be permeated with fine blood vessels and a thin coating of fat.

4. Breast of lamb

Lamb breast is a fatty joint with a good flavor. It requires long, slow, moist cooking and is, therefore, ideal for use in hearty soups. Breast of lamb can also be stuffed or rolled and then roasted.

CUTS

There are numerous ways to season or marinate lamb, and cooking methods include roasting, broiling, and braising. The first step when preparing lamb is to pull off the parchment-like skin.

2a. Filet of lamb

Lamb filet is the most expensive part of the loin and ranks with filet of beef and pork as one of the most highly regarded cuts. It is usually sold still attached to the loin chops. The best filet comes from young lambs and will be well-marbled with a fatty outer layer.

2b. Chuck

Cuts from the neck or chuck produce streaky, succulent meat that can be roasted, casseroled, and boiled. It is suitable for moist cooking, such as hearty soups, lamb and bean stew, ragoûts, or Irish Stew. Chuck is available rolled or unrolled.

5. Flank

This fatty cut is the most economical of all lamb cuts. It requires moist cooking and is suitable for use in hearty soups. Boned and rolled, it is also often roasted.

THE CORRECT WAY TO PREPARE AND COOK MEATS

The tenderness of cooked meats depends not so much on the quality of the meat but on the method used to cook it. However, meat can be made more tender if it is first marinated, tenderized, or pounded.

Cutlets, medallions, steaks, scallops, and rolled roasts are usually pounded.

Meat consists of fibers which are linked together in bundles and then surrounded by connective tissue. Pounding with a steak hammer shortens the fibers and tears the strands of connective tissue, so that when the meat is fried it retains its juices. If meat is not pounded, when it is heated the connective tissues contract and the juices flow out leaving the meat both tough and dry. Pounding also produces a uniform thickness, so the slices cook evenly.

When preparing meat, such as steaks, cutlets, and scallops, for frying or broiling, it is important to slit any fatty tissues or gristle with a sharp knife, otherwise the surface will curl.

Tenderizing is a process sometimes used in professional kitchens and restaurants. The steak or scallop is passed through a tenderizer – a machine with two wheel cutters which break down the connective tissue. This gives the impression that the meat is tender, but actually, much of the juice is lost, reducing the cooking time by about a half. Like ground meats, tenderized meats must be eaten on the day of purchase.

Marinating. Steaks and other small cuts are often marinated, a process requiring a seasoned liquid, such as vinegar, wine, oil, butter, or sour milk. The meat is left to soak in the liquid and the tannic and lactic acid bacteria loosen the connective tissues, the meat relaxes, and becomes more tender. In addition, cooking times are reduced and the shelf life of the meat extended by four to five days. Frozen meat should not be marinated, as the cell structure is damaged by the freezing process and the meat juices are lost.

The marinade is often used in the preparation of the sauce.

Tenderizing agents, such as papain, have the effect of destroying protein enzymes. (Papain is found in papaya and pineapple.) Hundreds of years ago, the natives of tropical countries noticed the meat-tenderizing properties of these fruits. Some chemically-produced tenderizing agents are now available, but no additives can replace the natural process of meat maturation.

Barding is used to protect lean meat from drying out and hardening around the outside.

Fresh, unsmoked pork back fat is required. This should be cut into thin strips, laid over the meat, usually in a lattice pattern, and then held in place with trussing thread. The fatty strips should be removed after roasting.

Larding is similar to barding. Pork fat is cut into 2–3-inch strips, then inserted into the outer surface of the meat joint with a trussing needle. About ⅛ inch of fat should be exposed at each end. Inevitably the meat cells are damaged and so barding is preferable to larding.

Deep-frying in batter is a method suitable for raw or cooked variety meats, either sliced or whole. Some types of sliced meats are also suitable for this cooking method. Meat for deep frying should be seasoned, dipped in a coating and then fried at about 340°F. Coatings containing wine or beer may be used for deep frying.

Coating with breadcrumbs is ideal not only for thin slices of meat or variety meats, but also for pieces of cooked meat coated in a sauce.

To coat a scallop, for example, season the meat with salt and pepper, dip first in flour, then in beaten egg, and coat in dry breadcrumbs before frying.

Grated cheese, ground almonds or other nuts, herbs, or shredded coconut can be added to the breadcrumbs.

Oven-roasting is advisable only for meats that are low in connective tissue, such as sirloin, fillet of beef, loin of veal, lamb or pork, and some cuts from the leg or shoulder of lamb, pork, or veal.

Relatively high cooking temperatures are required for this method. The meat is placed in hot fat and seared initially at 425–475°F, and then finished at 300–400°F. Heat the roasting pan in a pre-heated oven or on the stovetop, add the fat, and then the seasoned meat. After a few minutes turn the meat so that it browns all over.

As soon as it is well browned, lower the heat, and continue to cook at the lower temperature. The juices should not be allowed to escape, as the meat will then braise rather than roast. It is a good idea to baste the joint with hot fat from time to time.

You can test whether a joint is cooked by using a meat thermometer. The internal temperature of red meat, such as beef or lamb, should reach 100–120°F. For medium-roasted veal and pork, however, the meat thermometer should register 160–170°F. When the meat is cooked, leave it to rest on a cooling rack. Then, none of the valuable juices will be lost when it is carved and the process will also be easier.

Roasting with a fan-assisted oven. A fan circulates the hot air inside the oven which shortens cooking times. The oven temperature can be reduced and the meat roasts to a uniform brown.

Spit-roasting is a simple, straightforward, and healthy way of cooking meat. It is suitable not just for whole roasts, but also for whole animals, saddles, and thighs. Filets and sirloin may also be cooked on a rotisserie spit.

RARE, MEDIUM, AND WELL DONE SIRLOIN STEAK

As sirloin is not a compact meat, it is impossible to give strict cooking times. Broiling or frying times depend not only on the weight, but also the thickness of the steak. A professional rule of thumb is that 2 pounds of meat require 15 minutes.

1. Rare steaks are red inside a thin layer of cooked meat.

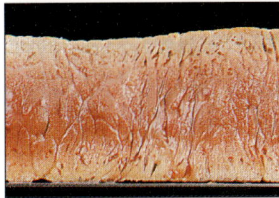

2. Medium steaks are a paler red.

3. Well-done steak is evenly cooked all through.

Quick-frying is suitable for chops, medallions, steaks, scallops and strips. Lean meats and variety meats are usually cut into portions, seasoned to taste with salt and pepper, and fried all over in hot oil or fat. When frying meat, it is generally advisable to ensure that it is turned several times, so that the exposed side does not cook too quickly and the meat does not cook unevenly.

Good quality meat will not become tough if it is well seasoned before frying. Only meat of inferior quality, that has not been cooked properly or has matured insufficiently will produce an unsatisfying meal.

Broiling, grilling, and barbecueing are healthy, tasty and low-fat methods of cooking meat. Cuts low in connective tissue are best suited to these methods. Very little juice is lost, as the meat cooks quickly at very high temperatures (575–650°F) and is quickly sealed.

Make sure that you preheat the broiler, grill, or barbecue. Thin slices of meat need be turned only once so that they do not dry out. Thicker steaks or chops, on the other hand, need to be turned twice, so that the characteristic lattice pattern is branded on the meat.

Make sure that the raw meat is salted and seasoned, brushed with oil and cooked at once. Finely-chopped herbs and garlic may be added to the oil to give extra flavor.

Meats and variety meats should not be pierced with a fork during broiling, grilling, or barbecuing. Instead, turn with a pair of tongs.

Steaming is mainly used for preparing light dishes. Little fat or liquid is required to cook food by this method, and veal which remains a pale color is the obvious choice.

First melt a little butter or margarine in the top part of the steamer, add the seasoned meat and turn it once. As soon as the meat has lost its raw flesh color, cover the saucepan, adding a little water if necessary.

For successful steaming, maintain a temperature of about 212°F within the covered steamer.

Braising consists first of searing meat to create the necessary coloring and flavor, and then completing the cooking by adding liquid to a dish that is then covered.

The ideal meat for braising comes from the thigh or shoulder and has a relatively high proportion of connective tissue. Whole cuts, cubed meats, and knuckle slices are normally braised. The meat is often marinated before cooking, but should be well drained before browning. Season the meat and fry it all over in hot oil or fat. Fried vegetables, such as carrots and onions, and a little tomato paste may then be added. Return the water or the marinade to the dish, cover and simmer, stirring from time to time.

Braised topside of veal.

Blanching simply means immersing food first in boiling water and then plunging it straight into cold water or refreshing it under cold running water. A few types of variety meats need to be blanched.

Boiling is, strictly speaking, cooking in water or broth at a temperature of 212°F. In fact, a slightly lower temperature of 185°–200°F is preferable. The best cuts of meat for boiling are those with dense connective tissue, such as knuckle, breast, thigh, or shoulder. Calf's head or variety meats, such as tongue and heart, can also be cooked in this way.

The golden rule has always been to make good broth, add the meat to cold water, but to make good meat add it to hot water. However, research by food scientists has demonstrated the opposite. The constituents of a broth are the same, whether the meat is added hot or cold, but if meat for boiling is added to cold water, the meat enzymes will develop better.

As a rule, meat is boiled uncovered. Herbs and vegetables are usually added for the last 35 minutes of the cooking time, and can then be used to flavor sauces and gravies.

Meat should never be boiled for too long, otherwise it may become dry and stringy.

CUTTING VEAL

1. For recipes requiring thin strips of veal, first cut a piece of rump into 1-inch cubes and then slice thinly.

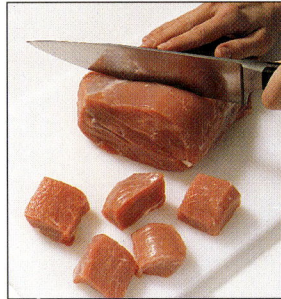

2. For veal stews, braised veal or goulash, cut the meat into 1½-inch slices, then into strips about the same width, and finally into cubes each weighing about 1½oz.

BROILING VEAL CUTLETS

1. Scrape the meat away from the rib tips.
2. Flatten each cutlet with a steak hammer. Pounding the meat shortens the fibers and tears the strands of connective tissue so the cutlet does not buckle during cooking.
3. Mix together dried herbs, such as sage, basil, thyme, or oregano, and a little oil.

Season the cutlets with salt and pepper, and dip them in the herb oil.
4. Place the cutlets on a pre-heated broiler pan.
5. Turn the cutlets over using tongs. If rotated a quarter of a turn, they will be branded with the characteristic lattice pattern.

1.

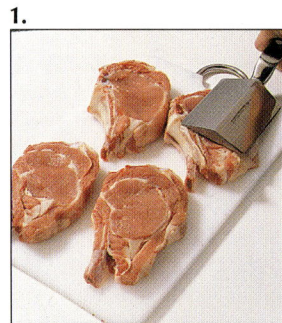
3.

2.

4.

5.

CARVING VEAL KNUCKLE

1. Hold a roasted knuckle of veal by the bone wrapped in a kitchen towel. Hold upright, and loosen the meat from the bone with a knife.

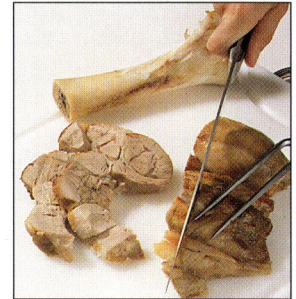

2. Using a fork to steady it, carve the veal into ½-inch slices on a chopping board.

PREPARING CALF'S SWEETBREADS

1. Remove any fibers or blood vessels with a knife.

2. Leave the sweetbreads to soak in cold water for several hours, changing the water frequently.

3. When the sweetbreads are white and the water remains clear, drain, and transfer to a pot of fresh, lightly salted water. Bring to the boil, and simmer for 3–4 minutes.

4. Plunge the sweetbreads into cold water and set aside to cool.

5. Return the sweetbreads to the pot, cover with cold water and cook according to the recipe.

6. When cooked, trim off any remaining skin and cut the sweetbreads into ¼-inch slices.

7. If the sweetbreads are required for a stew or a soup, each section must be carefully separated from the connecting tissue.

PREPARING CALF'S LIVER

1. Place the calf's liver in tepid water for 2–3 minutes.

2. If necessary, loosen the skin; push the thumb underneath and pull the skin off.

3. Starting at the thicker side, cut diagonally away from the flat side to make pencil-thick slices.

4. Sprinkle the liver slices with salt and pepper.

5. Dip the liver slices in flour and shake off any excess.

6. Melt a little butter in a skillet, and gently fry the liver slices.

7. Use the prongs of a fork to turn the liver over two or three times until it is pale pink inside.

3.

4.

5.

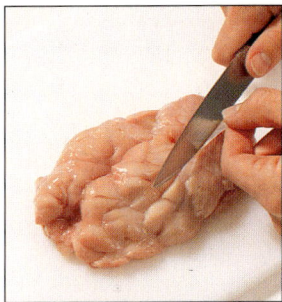

1.

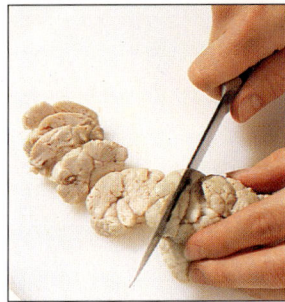

2.

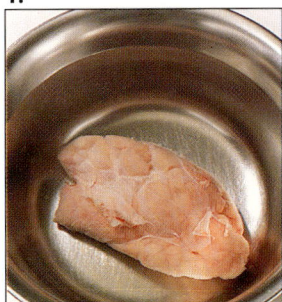

6.

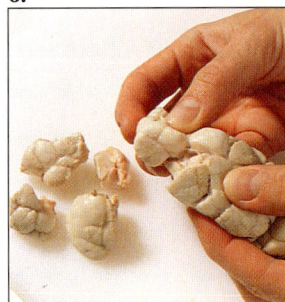

7.

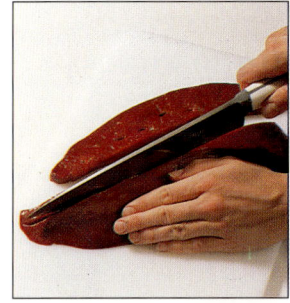

3.

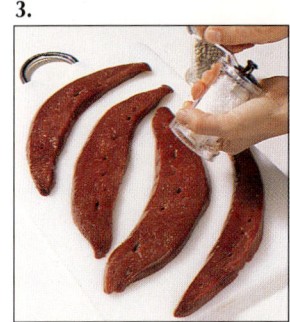

4.

5.

1.

2.

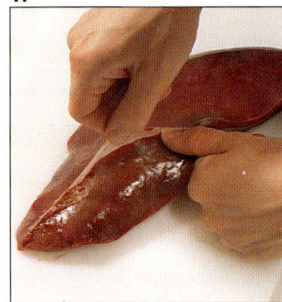

6.

7.

PREPARING PIG'S KIDNEYS

1. Remove the skin from the kidneys and lay them flat on a chopping board. Cut each kidney in half horizontally.

2. Use a knife with a sharp point to remove the white core from inside the kidney.

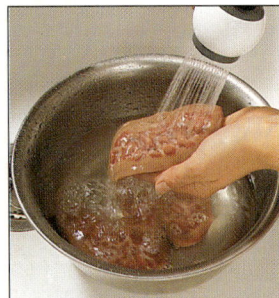

3. Rinse the kidneys thoroughly and pat dry. Pig's kidneys may also be blanched.
To fry kidneys, cut each halved kidney into ¼-inch slices.

PREPARING ROAST PORK WITH CRISP CRACKLING

1. Place a 2¼–2¾lb pork joint, rind downward, in a large pan of cold water. To prevent the rind buckling, boil for a few minutes.

2. Use a sharp knife to cut a lattice pattern in the rind. These cuts allow the fat to escape during roasting. Rub salt into the flesh.

3. Cover a roasting pan with water to a depth of ¼ inch. Place the pork roast in the pan, rind downward. Add a few bones if available.

4. Sprinkle some caraway seeds over the meat, if liked, cover with a lid, and roast in a preheated oven at 400°F for 25 minutes or until sufficient fat has emerged.

5. Remove the lid and turn the joint over so that the rind is uppermost. Cook for a further 40–45 minutes, allowing the remaining water to evaporate.

6. From time to time, baste with fat, and brush the rind with a little beer.

7. About 35 minutes before the end of the roasting time, add a peeled and diced onion and carrot.

8. Place the cooked roast on a cooling rack, pour off the fat, and make a sauce with water or meat broth.

9. To make the gravy, mix together a little water and cornstarch to make a smooth paste. Stir into the sauce to thicken. Strain and season to taste.

10. Cut the roast pork into slices and serve with the sauce.

1.

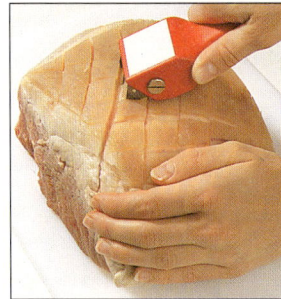

2.

3.

4.

5.

6.

7.

8.

9.

10.

Hearty Home Cooking

*S*unday lunch, the aroma of roast beef – home cooking's finest hour when delicious helpings of meat form the focal point for the family gathering. Yet it is the rich, tasty sauces and gravies that accompany roast beef, pork, and veal that often prove to be the highlight. Many of the recipes included in this section have been passed down from generation to generation, and it is here that their appeal lies. However, many new recipes have also been included, offering opportunities for serious home cooks to develop and extend their repertoires.

Spicy Meatloaf
(recipe page 28)

BEEF OLIVES

SERVES 4
Preparation and cooking time: 1½ hours
Kcal per serving: 455
P = 36g, F = 30g, C = 5g

4 x 5–6 ounce slices lean beef
salt
freshly ground black pepper
2 tbsps hot made mustard
4 thin slices bacon, rinded
3 onions
2 small pickles
4 rosemary sprigs
1 tbsp vegetable oil
1 tbsp butter
1 carrot
1 stick celery
2 tomatoes
1 tbsp dried mushrooms, soaked
½ bayleaf
4 black peppercorns
1 cup beef broth
½ cup red wine
4 tbsps sour cream

Season the beef olives, add the filling, and then roll up from the narrow end.

Secure each beef olive with a cocktail stick or trussing thread.

1. Press the slices of beef with the flat edge of a kitchen knife or with your hands to flatten. Sprinkle with pepper and coat with mustard. Lay a slice of bacon on top of each slice of beef.
2. Peel and chop the onions. Quarter the gherkins lengthwise. Finely chop or crush the rosemary leaves. Divide one third of the chopped onion between the beef slices. Place 2 pieces of gherkin on each roulade, sprinkle with the rosemary, and roll up tightly from the narrow end. Secure each roll with a trussing thread or a cocktail stick. Heat the oil and butter in a flameproof casserole, and fry the roulades over a high heat until browned on all sides.
3. Peel the carrot and cut into matchstick strips. Trim the celery and cut into matchstick strips. Blanch, skin, and chop the tomatoes. Add the remaining onion, carrot, celery, and tomatoes to the casserole, and cook over a low heat for a further

5 minutes. Add the soaked mushrooms, bayleaf, and peppercorns. Pour in the wine and broth, cover and braise for 1½ hours over a low heat.
4. Remove the beef olives. Strain the cooking liquid and rub it through a sieve or purée in a blender. Return to the pan, add the sour cream, bring to the boil, and reduce slightly. Season to taste with salt and pepper. Return the beef olives to the sauce to reheat. Transfer to a serving dish, remove the cocktail sticks or trussing thread, and serve.
Serving suggestions: roast potatoes and Brussels sprouts.
Recommended drink: a medium red wine.

SPICY MEATLOAF

(photograph page 26)

SERVES 4–6
Preparation and cooking time: 1 hour
Kcal per serving if serving 4: 670
P = 38g, F = 45g, C = 29g

4 ounces ham steak
14 ounces ground beef
2 tbsps grated Swiss cheese
¼ tsp cinnamon
2 eggs, lightly beaten
3 tbsps breadcrumbs, soaked in milk
juice of 1 lemon
salt
freshly ground black pepper
6 tbsps vegetable oil
4 tbsps breadcrumbs
1 onion
1 carrot
1 stick celery
4 tomatoes
6 tbsps light cream

1. Finely chop the ham steaks or finely grind in a food processor. Mix together the ham, ground beef, cheese, cinnamon, eggs, breadcrumbs, and lemon juice, and season to taste with salt and pepper. Knead well to make a smooth mixture. Shape the mixture into a loaf.
2. Heat the oil in a flameproof casserole. Dip the meatloaf in the breadcrumbs to coat. Fry the meatloaf until browned all over.
3. Peel and chop the onion and carrot. Trim and slice the celery. Add the onion, carrot, and celery to the casserole, and fry for a further 5 minutes. Blanch, skin, and chop the tomatoes. Add the tomatoes to the casserole, and season to taste with salt and pepper.
4. Bake the meatloaf in a preheated oven at 400°F for about 30 minutes. Remove from the dish and keep warm.

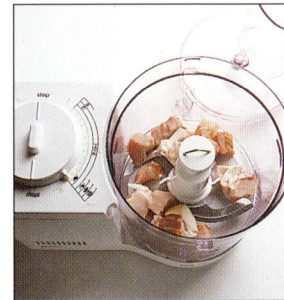
Grind the ham steak by hand or in a food processor.

Fry the finely chopped vegetables with the meatloaf before baking.

5. Add 4 tbsps water to the cooking juices, stir in the cream, and heat through. Rub the sauce through a sieve and serve separately. Alternatively, retain the vegetables and pour the sauce over the meatloaf.
Serving suggestions: boiled potatoes with parsley and assorted baby vegetables.
Recommended drinks: chilled beer, cider or a dry, white wine.

> **TIP**
>
> *Meatloaf can be cooked in a cooking brick, an unglazed earthware pot. The pot must be soaked in water for 2 hours and the oven must not be preheated.*

FILET STEAK WITH ONIONS

SERVES 4 ■

*Preparation and cooking
time: 20 minutes
Marinate overnight
Kcal per serving: 610
P = 42g, F = 47g, C = 4g*

*4 x 7 ounce filet steaks
6 tbsps olive oil
4 onions
2 tbsps butter
salt
freshly ground black pepper*

1. Flatten the steaks slightly by pressing them with the heel of your hand. Place in a large, shallow dish and pour 5 tbsps of the oil over them. Set them aside to marinate overnight. Turn the steaks over from time to time.
2. Peel and slice the onions. Heat the remaining oil and the butter, and fry the onions until transparent. Remove from the pan and keep warm.
3. Drain the steaks and pat dry. Fry the steaks in the same pan for 4 minutes. Turn, season with salt and pepper, and fry for a further 4 minutes. Remove from the pan and transfer to a warm serving dish. Top each steak with fried onions and serve immediately.
Serving suggestions: green beans tossed in butter, broiled tomatoes, and buttered potatoes.
Recommended drinks: beer or a young, strong red wine.

Pour 5 tbsps oil over the steaks and set aside to marinate.

Chop the onions and fry them in the butter and oil until transparent.

Fry the steaks in the onion-flavored oil until browned on both sides.

PEPPERED STEAKS

SERVES 4 ■

*Preparation and cooking
time: 15-20 minutes
Kcal per serving: 360
P = 39g, F = 18g, C = 2g*

*4 x 7–8 ounce filet or sirloin
  steaks
2 tbsps coarsely crushed
  black peppercorns
1 tbsp oil
1 tbsp butter
salt
4 tsps brandy
2 shallots
½ cup beef broth
½ cup white wine
4 tbsps sour cream
2 tbsps garden cress*

1. Dry the steaks with kitchen paper and press the crushed peppercorns into the meat. Push down hard with the heel of your hand so that the pepper becomes embedded.
2. Heat the oil and butter in a skillet, and fry the steaks for 3–4 minutes on each side until well browned. Warm the brandy in a small pan. Pour the brandy over the steaks, ignite, and shake the pan until the flames die down. Remove the steaks from the pan and keep warm.
3. Peel and chop the shallots. Mix together the shallots, meat broth, and wine, and bring to the boil in a small pan. Reduce to a third. Pour the broth and wine mixture into the skillet, and scrape the base of the pan to deglaze. Beat in the sour cream over a medium heat until thick and creamy. Pour the sauce over the steaks and garnish with the cress.
Serving suggestions: mixed salad with French fries or crusty French bread.
Recommended drink: a medium red wine.

Press the crushed peppercorns firmly into the steaks.

Flambé the fried steaks with a little warmed brandy.

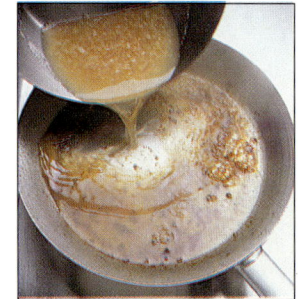
Deglaze the skillet with wine and broth.

Add the sour cream and then reduce the sauce until it thickens, beating constantly.

VEAL OLIVES

SERVES 4 ■■

*Preparation and cooking
time: 1½ hours
Kcal per serving: 470
P = 42g, F = 29g, C = 5g*

4 x 5½ ounce long veal
   scallops
salt
freshly ground black pepper
2 thin slices raw ham
1 tbsp vegetable oil
2 tbsps butter
1 onion
1 carrot
1 stick celery
fresh pork rind
3 sage leaves
½ cup white wine
½ cup beef broth

FOR THE FILLING:
1 tbsp butter
1 tbsp chopped shallots
½ cup mushrooms
⅔ cup sausagemeat
1 tsp minced parsley
1 egg yolk
1 tbsp breadcrumbs
pinch of dried thyme
salt
freshly ground black pepper

*Blend the sausagemeat and
mushrooms in a food processor,
then add the parsley, egg yolk,
breadcrumbs, and seasoning.*

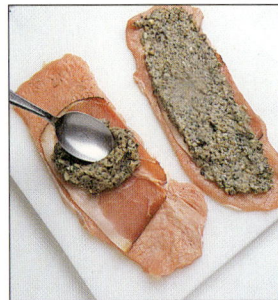

*Place a slice of ham on each slice
of veal and spread the filling on
the top.*

1. Flatten the scallops with the heel of your hand. Rub in a little salt and pepper.
2. To make the filling, melt the butter and fry the shallots until transparent. Chop the mushrooms. Place the mushrooms and sausagemeat in a food processor and work briefly. Add the parsley, egg yolk, breadcrumbs, thyme, and salt and pepper, and blend. Add the sausagemeat mixture to the shallots.
3. Cut the slices of ham in half lengthwise. Cover each scallop with a strip of the ham and spread the filling on top. Roll up the scallop and secure with trussing thread or cocktail sticks.
4. Heat the oil and half the butter, and fry the veal olives until browned all over. Peel and slice the onion and carrot. Trim the celery and cut into matchstick strips. Add the onion, carrot, and celery to the pan, and fry for a further 5 minutes. Add the pork rind, sage, wine, and broth, cover, and cook for 45 minutes.
5. Transfer the veal olives to a serving dish and keep warm. Drain the sauce and rub through a sieve. Return to the pan, bring to the boil, and allow to reduce a little. Stir in the remaining butter. Pour the sauce over the veal olives and serve immediately.
Serving suggestions: mashed potato and baby carrots.
Recommended drink: a fruity white wine.

BRAISED KNUCKLE OF VEAL

SERVES 4 ■

*Preparation and cooking
time: 1¾ hours
Kcal per serving: 475
P = 83g, F = 11g, C = 5g*

1 knuckle of veal (about 3½
   pounds)
salt
freshly ground white pepper
2 tbsps butter
8 ounces pork belly with rind
1 large onion
2 carrots
½ bayleaf
2 cloves
rind of 1 lemon
½ cup white wine
1 cup beef broth
2 tomatoes

1. Wash the knuckle of veal and pat dry. Rub in salt and pepper. Melt the butter in a Dutch oven, and fry the veal and pork belly until browned on all sides.
2. Peel and slice the onion and carrots. Add the onion and carrots to the casserole, and fry for a further 5 minutes. Add the bayleaf, cloves, and lemon rind and pour in the wine and broth. Blanch, skin, and chop the tomatoes. Add the tomatoes to the casserole, and season to taste with salt and pepper.
3. Cover and cook in a preheated oven at 400°F for 1¼ hours. Remove the lid and return the casserole to the oven for a further 15 minutes, basting the veal with the liquid from time to time.
4. Remove the veal and pork from the pot and keep warm. If necessary, brown the belly of pork in a hot oven. Rub the cooking liquid through a sieve and pour off the fat. Cut the veal into slices. Remove the rind from the pork and cut the meat into slices. Arrange the veal and pork together on a serving dish and hand the gravy separately.
Serving suggestions: dumplings, peas, and carrots.
Recommended drink: a young, fruity white wine.

*Brown the veal and pork in the
melted butter.*

*Add the chopped carrots and
onion.*

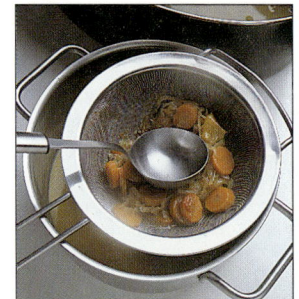

*To make the gravy, rub the liquid
through a fine sieve.*

BRAISED CALVES' HEARTS

SERVES 4 ■
Preparation and cooking time:
30 minutes
Kcal per serving: 450
P = 29g, F = 28g, C = 4g

2 x calves' hearts (about 14 ounces each)
salt
freshly ground white pepper
1 tbsp oil
1 tbsp butter

FOR THE SAUCE:
2-3 shallots
⅔ cup fresh mushrooms
1 small carrot
1 stick celery
3 tbsps butter
½ cup dry white wine
4 tbsps sour cream

1. Wash the calves' hearts and pat dry. Cut them in half and remove any skin, and gristle. Season well.
2. Heat the oil and butter in a skillet, and fry the hearts until well browned all over. Cover, and cook over a low heat for 10 minutes.
3. To make the sauce, peel and finely chop the shallots. Slice the mushrooms. Peel and chop the carrot. Trim and chop the celery.
4. Melt the butter in a small skillet, and gently fry the shallots, mushrooms, carrot, and celery for 10 minutes. Add the white wine, bring to the boil, and allow to reduce slightly. Stir in the sour cream. Reduce the sauce again slightly.
5. Cut the heart into thin slices. They should still be a delicate pink inside. Arrange on a warm serving plate, and pour over the sauce.
You could substitute pigs' hearts (about 1¾ pounds).
Serving suggestions: noodles and salad.
Recommended drink: medium-dry white wine.

CALF'S LIVER WITH APPLES

SERVES 4 ■
Preparation and cooking time: 30 minutes
Kcal per serving: 385
P = 27g, F = 23g, C = 19g

4 x slices calf's liver (about 5 ounces each)
2 large onions
2 tart apples
1 tbsp all-purpose flour
salt
freshly ground black pepper
1 tbsp oil
3 tbsps butter
4 thin slices bacon, rinded

1. Remove any skin and membranes from the liver. Starting at the thicker side, cut diagonally away from the flat side to make pencil-thin slices.
2. Peel and thinly slice the onions and push out into rings. Peel, core, and slice the apples into rings. Season the flour with salt and pepper.
3. Heat the oil and 1 tbsp of the butter in a skillet, and fry the bacon until crisp. Remove from the pan. Coat the liver with the seasoned flour, and fry for about 5 minutes turning once, until golden-brown on both sides.
4. Melt the remaining butter in a second skillet. Fry the apple slices until soft. Remove from the pan and keep warm. Fry the onion rings in the same pan.
5. Season the fried liver with pepper and arrange on a warm serving dish. Serve topped with the apple slices, onion rings, and crisp bacon.
Serving suggestion: mashed potato.
Recommended drinks: cider or chilled beer.

Core the apples and then cut them into rings ½ inch thick.

Brown the liver on both sides.

Fry the apple slices in a separate skillet until soft.

KIDNEYS WITH MUSTARD SAUCE

SERVES 4 ■
Preparation and cooking time: 30 minutes
Soaking time: 1 hour
Kcal per serving: 350
P = 22g, F = 27g, C = 3g

2 x large calves' or lamb kidneys (about 1 pound each)
salt
freshly ground black pepper
2 tbsps butter
1 small onion
⅔ cup sour cream
1 tbsp finely grated fresh root ginger
1 tbsp French or American mustard
2 tbsps snipped fresh chives

1. Core the kidneys and discard any membrane and skin. Place them in a bowl, cover with cold water and soak for 1 hour. Drain the kidneys, wash well, and pat dry. Rub pepper into the flesh. Melt half the butter in a skillet, and fry the kidneys all over for about 10 minutes. When all the liquid has evaporated season with salt.
2. Peel and chop the onion. Melt the remaining butter in a second pan, and gently fry the onion until transparent. Add the sour cream and ginger, and season lightly with salt. Allow to reduce slightly, stirring frequently.
3. Remove the kidneys from the pan and slice thinly. Transfer to a warm serving dish.
4. Pour the cooking juices into a small pan, and stir in the mustard and ginger cream. Heat through, and season to taste with salt and pepper.
5. Pour the hot sauce over the kidneys, sprinkle with the chives, and serve.
Serving suggestions: mushrooms and roast potatoes.
Recommended drink: a full-bodied red wine.

HAM IN A LOAF

SERVES 6

Preparation and cooking time: 2½ hours
Soaking time: about 12 hours
Kcal per serving: 890
P = 62g, F = 38g, C = 75g

1 Smithfield ham (about 3
    pounds)
2½ pounds bread or pizza
    dough (homemade or
    prepared from a mix)
1 egg yolk
2 tbsps butter

Roll out the dough to ½ inch thick. Place rinded ham in the center of the dough.

1. Place the ham in a deep dish, cover with cold water and set aside overnight to soak.
2. Transfer the ham to a large pan and cover with fresh water. Bring to the boil and simmer for 1 hour. Remove the ham from the pan and remove the rind.
3. Butter a roasting pan or baking sheet.
4. Roll out the dough, on a lightly-floured surface, to about ½ inch thick. Place the ham in the center and carefully wrap the dough around it to form a secure parcel. Beat the egg yolk with 1 tsp water and brush the surface of the dough with this glaze. Prick the dough in several places with a fork.
5. Transfer the ham parcel to the roasting pan or baking sheet. Bake in a preheated oven at 375°F for 1½ hours. Leave to cool for 10 minutes before cutting into thick slices.
Serving suggestion: horseradish sauce.
Recommended drink: chilled beer.

Wrap the dough around the ham so that none of the meat juices can escape.

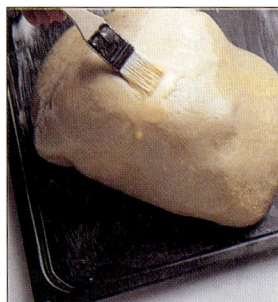

Before baking, brush the dough with a mixture of egg yolk and water.

> **TIP**
>
> *Any ham leftovers taste delicious with Cumberland sauce.*

PICKLED HAM KNUCKLE

SERVES 4

Preparation and cooking time: 2½ hours
Kcal per serving: 485
P = 29g, F = 42g, C = 0g

1 knuckle of ham (about 3½
    pounds)
salt
1 large onion
1 bunch herbs
1 bayleaf
5 white peppercorns

1. Wash the ham in plenty of cold salted water. Place in a large pan, cover with water, and bring to the boil. Skim off the froth. Peel and halve the onion. Add the onion, herbs, bayleaf and peppercorns to the pan. Cook for 2–2½ hours over a low heat. When the ham is cooked it will come easily away from the bone.
2. Remove the ham from the pan and serve. The bone may be very big and you may prefer to remove it and serve the ham cut into slices.
Serving suggestions: cooked spring vegetables, cabbage, and mashed potatoes.
Recommended drinks: beer or rosé wine.

> **TIP**
>
> *The knuckle can also be cooked on sauerkraut. Small, cured pig's feet also make an appetizing dish.*

LOIN OF PORK WITH CHERRY SAUCE

SERVES 4

Preparation and cooking time: 25 minutes
Kcal per serving: 415
P = 29g, F = 29g, C = 10g

12 x slices pork filet (about 2
    ounces each) or 4 boneless
    loin chops
salt
1 tsp ground ginger
1 tbsp vegetable oil
1 tbsp butter
6 tbsps canned Morello
    cherries, pitted
1 tbsp sugar
½ cup broth
4 tbsps sour cream

1. Rub the pork slices with a little salt and a little ginger. Heat the oil and butter, and fry the meat on both sides until well browned.
2. Drain the cherries and reserve the juice. Fry the cherries with the sugar in a skillet, stirring constantly, until the sugar begins to caramelize.
3. Pour the broth into the pan and bring to the boil. Add the reserved cherry juice, heat through, and allow to reduce slightly. Stir in the sour cream and reheat. Season with a little ginger.
4. Arrange the meat on a serving dish, and pour a little of the cherry sauce over it. Serve the remaining sauce separately.
This dish tastes marvellous if fresh Morello cherries are used.
Serving suggestion: potato croquettes.
Recommended drink: medium dry white wine.

SPICY MEATBALLS

SERVES 4 ■
Preparation and cooking time: 30 minutes
Kcal per serving: 370
P = 31g, F = 24g, C = 6g

1 onion
8 ounces finely ground veal or beef
8 ounces finely ground pork
3 tbsps all-purpose flour or breadcrumbs
salt
freshly ground black pepper
1 egg
⅓ cup milk or bottled water
1 ounce butter

Add sufficient milk to the meat and flour or breadcrumbs to make a light, workable mixture.

Use 2 wet spoons to shape the meatballs, and to place them in the hot butter.

Fry the meatballs over a low heat until they are brown all over.

1. Peel and mince or grate the onion. Mix together the onion, ground meats and the flour or breadcrumbs, and season to taste with salt and pepper. Add the egg and milk or bottled water to the meat and knead well until the mixture is light and easily workable.
2. Melt the butter in a skillet. Use wet hands or 2 spoons dipped in water and make small meatballs. Shape them either into balls or flat burgers, and fry them over a low heat until golden-brown all over.
Serving suggestions: potatoes, red cabbage, or spinach.
Recommended drinks: beer or young red wine.

SPINACH ROLLS

SERVES 4 ■
Preparation and cooking time: 50 minutes
Kcal per serving: 290
P = 14g, F = 22g, C = 8g

16 large spinach leaves
1 day-old bread roll or 2 thick slices white bread
1 onion
3 tbsps butter
1 tbsp minced parsley
8 ounces sausagemeat
1 egg
pinch freshly grated nutmeg
½ cup broth
2 tbsps sour cream (optional)

1. Blanch each spinach leaf separately in boiling water for a few seconds. Spread the leaves out on a board. Tear the roll or bread into pieces, place in a bowl, and cover with water. Set aside to soak. Peel and finely chop the onion. Melt 1 tbsp of the butter, and fry the onion and parsley for 5 minutes.
2. Squeeze the water from the roll or bread. Mix together the sausagemeat, roll or bread, egg, and the onion-and-parsley mixture. Knead thoroughly and season with a little nutmeg. Place 2 spinach leaves together, spoon a little of the filling into the center and roll up, keeping the leaf ends facing downward. Repeat until the ingredients are used up.
3. Melt the remaining butter, and fry the spinach rolls all over. Add the broth, cover, and simmer for 20–30 minutes. If liked, add the sour cream just before serving to thicken the sauce.
These spinach rolls make an excellent appetizer served with crusty white bread.
Serving suggestion: mashed potato.
Recommended drink: a medium white wine.

PORK CHOPS WITH PAPRIKA SAUCE

SERVES 4 ■
Preparation and cooking time: 15 minutes
Kcal per serving: 515
P = 26g, F = 41g, C = 10g

4 pork chops (about 6 ounces each)
salt
2 tbsps all-purpose flour
1 tbsp butter
1 tbsp oil
1 large onion
2 garlic cloves
2 tsps sweet paprika
2 tbsps tomato paste
1 cup sour cream

1. Rub the pork chops with a little salt, and dip in the flour. Heat the butter and oil in a skillet, and fry the chops for 10 minutes, turning once, until golden-brown. Remove from the pan and keep warm.
2. Peel and slice the onion. Peel and chop the garlic cloves. Fry the onion and garlic in the same pan for 5–7 minutes. Sprinkle with the paprika and stir in the tomato paste. Stir in the sour cream, and heat through. Return the chops to the pan and heat through for 2 minutes.
Serving suggestions: fettuccini and cucumber salad.
Recommended drinks: beer or Zinfandel.

TIP

To make the paprika sauce a little hotter, add a small red chili pepper to the onions, but remove it before serving.

Dishes from Around the World

*T*his chapter offers a selection of some of the best-known and most popular meat dishes from around the world, including specialties from French, Austrian, and Italian cuisines, as well as exotic dishes from China, Turkey, the Middle East, and India. This section provides a wealth of ideas, making it ideal for all adventurous cooks.

Cantonese Fondue
(recipe page 53)

BEEF WELLINGTON

SERVES 4 ■ ■
*Preparation and cooking
time: 1¼ hours
Kcal per serving: 870
P = 58g, F = 61g, C = 26g*

2½ pounds filet of beef
salt
freshly ground black pepper
4 tbsps butter
10 ounces frozen puff dough,
    thawed
1 egg yolk

FOR THE FILLING:
4 ounces ham
1 onion
⅔ cup mushrooms
1 tbsp minced parsley
4 tbsps butter

*Spread the filling in the middle of
the rolled-out dough.*

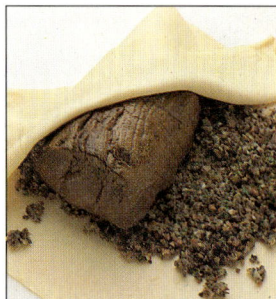
*Place the filet at one end of the
filling so that it will surround the
filet when the dough is folded.*

1. Rinse the meat and pat dry. Rub a little salt and pepper into the meat. Melt the butter in a roasting pan, and fry the beef filet all over. Roast in a preheated oven at 475°F for 30 minutes, basting frequently. The filet should remain red in the middle.
2. Lower oven temperature to 425°F.
3. Meanwhile, make the filling. Dice the ham. Peel and finely chop the onion. Finely chop the mushrooms. Melt the butter in a skillet, and gently fry the ham, onion, mushrooms, and parsley for 5–7 minutes. Set aside to cool.
4. Roll out the dough into a rectangle slightly longer than the filet and three times as wide. Spread the cooled filling in the center of the dough, place the beef on top, and wrap the dough around it. Roll up the open ends of the dough sheet and press lightly to ensure that none of the meat juices escape. Beat the egg yolk and brush over the dough. Decorate the top of the "parcel" with dough trimmings, if liked.

*Decorate the top of the "parcel"
with strips of dough and brush
with egg yolk.*

5. Rinse a baking sheet in cold water and place the "parcel" in the center. Bake for 35 minutes or until the pastry is golden-brown. Serve warm or cold.
Serving suggestions: serve hot with mixed vegetables or cold with a salad or Cumberland sauce.
Recommended drink: a mature, fruity red wine.

BOEUF BOURGUIGNON

Burgundy beef

SERVES 6 ■ ■
*Preparation and cooking
time: 3–4 hours
Marinate overnight
Kcal per serving: 485
P = 39g, F = 18g, C = 9g*

2½ pounds beef shoulder or
    rib
2 large onions
1 garlic clove
1 bottle robust red wine
1 bunch herbs
4 ounces bacon, rind
    removed
12 baby onions
1 tbsp sunflower oil
2 tbsps butter
2 carrots
salt
freshly ground black pepper
1 tbsp all-purpose flour
1 cup mushrooms
4 tsps brandy

1. Cut the beef into 1½-inch cubes. Peel and slice the large onions and the garlic. Place the meat in a dish with half the wine. Add the bunch of herbs, onions, and garlic, and set aside overnight to marinate.
2. Chop the bacon. Peel the baby onions. Heat the oil and half the butter in a flameproof casserole, and fry the bacon until the fat runs. Add the baby onions, and stir-fry until golden. Remove the onions and bacon with a slotted spoon and set aside to drain.
3. Drain the meat and reserve the marinade. Pat dry and fry, stirring frequently, until lightly browned all over. Peel and dice the carrots, and fry for 5 minutes. Season to taste, sprinkle with the flour, and fry for a further 2–3 minutes. Stir in the reserved marinade and wine and heat through.
4. Cover and simmer for 3–3½ hours.

*Set aside the meat and onions in
red wine to marinate overnight.*

*Fry the bacon until the fat runs,
add the baby onions, and cook
until golden-brown.*

5. Wipe the mushrooms. Melt the remaining butter, and gently fry the mushrooms until all the liquid has evaporated. Add the mushrooms, baby onions, and bacon to the casserole, and cook for a further 20 minutes over a low heat. Warm the brandy in a small pan. Pour over the meat, ignite, and shake the pan until the flames die down.
Serving suggestions: boiled potatoes and garden peas.
Recommended drink: the same type of red wine that was used for the marinade.

BŒUF À LA MODE

Braised beef French style

SERVES 6   ■ ■
*Preparation and cooking
time: 5½ hours
Marinate overnight
Kcal per serving: 540
P = 43g, F = 28g, C = 13g*

2½ pounds round or topside
    of beef
4 slices streaky bacon, rinds
    removed
4 tsps brandy
salt
freshly ground black pepper
pinch ground ginger
pinch freshly grated nutmeg
2 cups dry white wine
1 bunch herbs
1 calf's foot
1 piece pork rind
1 large carrot
4 tbsps butter or lard
1 onion, peeled and studded
    with 3 cloves
1 cup beef broth

TO SERVE:
4 cups carrots
16 baby onions
2 tbsps butter

1. Rinse the beef and pat
dry. Cut the bacon into
strips, dip them in 2 table-
spoons of brandy, sprinkle
with pepper, ginger, and nutmeg, and set aside for 30
minutes.
2. Lard the meat with the
bacon strips, inserting them
in the same direction as the
meat fibers. Rub salt and
pepper into the meat. Place
the meat in a small dish and
add the wine, the remaining
brandy, and the herbs and
set aside overnight to marinate.
3. Place the calf's foot and
pork rind in a large pan,
cover with cold water, and
bring to the boil. Remove
from the heat and set aside
to cool.
4. Peel the carrot. Melt the
butter or lard in a heavy, pan.
Drain the beef and pat dry.

Fry the beef until browned
all over. Add the calf's foot,
pork rind, carrot, and onion,
and fry for 10 minutes. Pour
in the marinade and broth,
and cover.
5. Simmer the beef for 4
hours over a low heat or
cook in a preheated oven at
350°F for 4 hours.
6. To prepare the dish for
serving, peel, and thickly
slice the carrots. Peel the
onions. Melt the butter, and
gently fry the onions and carrots until golden.
7. Remove the meat, calf's
foot, and pork rind from the
dish. Dice the calf's foot and
pork rind. Rub the sauce
through a sieve. (The vegetables in the sauce will help to
bind it.) If the sauce is too
thick, add a glass of wine.
Season to taste with salt.
Return the meat, sliced carrots, sauce, chopped calf's
foot, and pork rind to the
dish. Cover and cook gently
for a further hour.
8. Remove the meat and set
aside to stand, then cut into
slices. Skim any fat from the
sauce, and season again if
required. Arrange the meat
slices on a warm serving
dish, add the sauce and garnish with the vegetables and
pork rind. Alternatively,
carve the beef at the table.
Serving suggestion: baked
potatoes.
Recommended drink: the
same type of wine that was
used for the marinade.

ROAST BEEF AND YORKSHIRE PUDDING

SERVES 6–8   ■ ■
*Preparation and cooking
time: about 2 hours
Kcal per serving if serving 6:
480
P = 40g, F = 29g, C = 16g*

1 London broil or rib roast
    (about 3 pounds)
4 tbsps butter
salt
freshly ground black pepper
½ cup beef broth or wine

**FOR THE YORKSHIRE
PUDDING:**
2 eggs
1¼ cups flour
½ tsp salt
1 cup milk
2 tbsps beef fat or shortening

1. Rinse the beef and pat
dry. Melt the butter and
brush over the meat.
Sprinkle with pepper. Place
the meat in a large roasting
pan and roast in a preheated
oven at 425°F for 15 min-
utes. Lower the temperature
to 375°F. Season the meat
with salt, and pour the broth
or wine into the roasting
pan.
2. Roast the beef as follows:
allow 18 minutes per pound
for rare beef, 22–25 minutes
per pound for medium, and
30 minutes per pound for
well done.
3. To make the Yorkshire
pudding, beat the eggs. Sift
the flour and salt into a bowl
and make a well in the center. Gradually beat in the
eggs and ½ cup of the milk.
Add the remaining milk and
beat to form a smooth, thin
mix. Cover and leave to
stand in a cool place for 1
hour.
4. About 30 minutes before
the beef is ready, melt the
lard or dripping in a large
rectangular roasting pan or a
muffin pan for individual
portions. Beat the mixture

*Before roasting, brush melted
butter over the beef joint, and
sprinkle generously with pepper.*

and pour into the pan or
muffin cups. Place on the
top shelf of the oven and
cook for 25 minutes or until
well-risen and golden-
brown.
5. Remove the meat from
the oven and set aside on a
warm dish to stand for 15
minutes. To make the gravy,
combine the meat juices
with a little water and heat
through. Cut the Yorkshire
pudding into portions with a
sharp knife or remove the
individual puddings from the
pan and serve with the beef.
Serving suggestion: garden
peas or cabbage.
Recommended drink: a
mature red wine or Guiness.

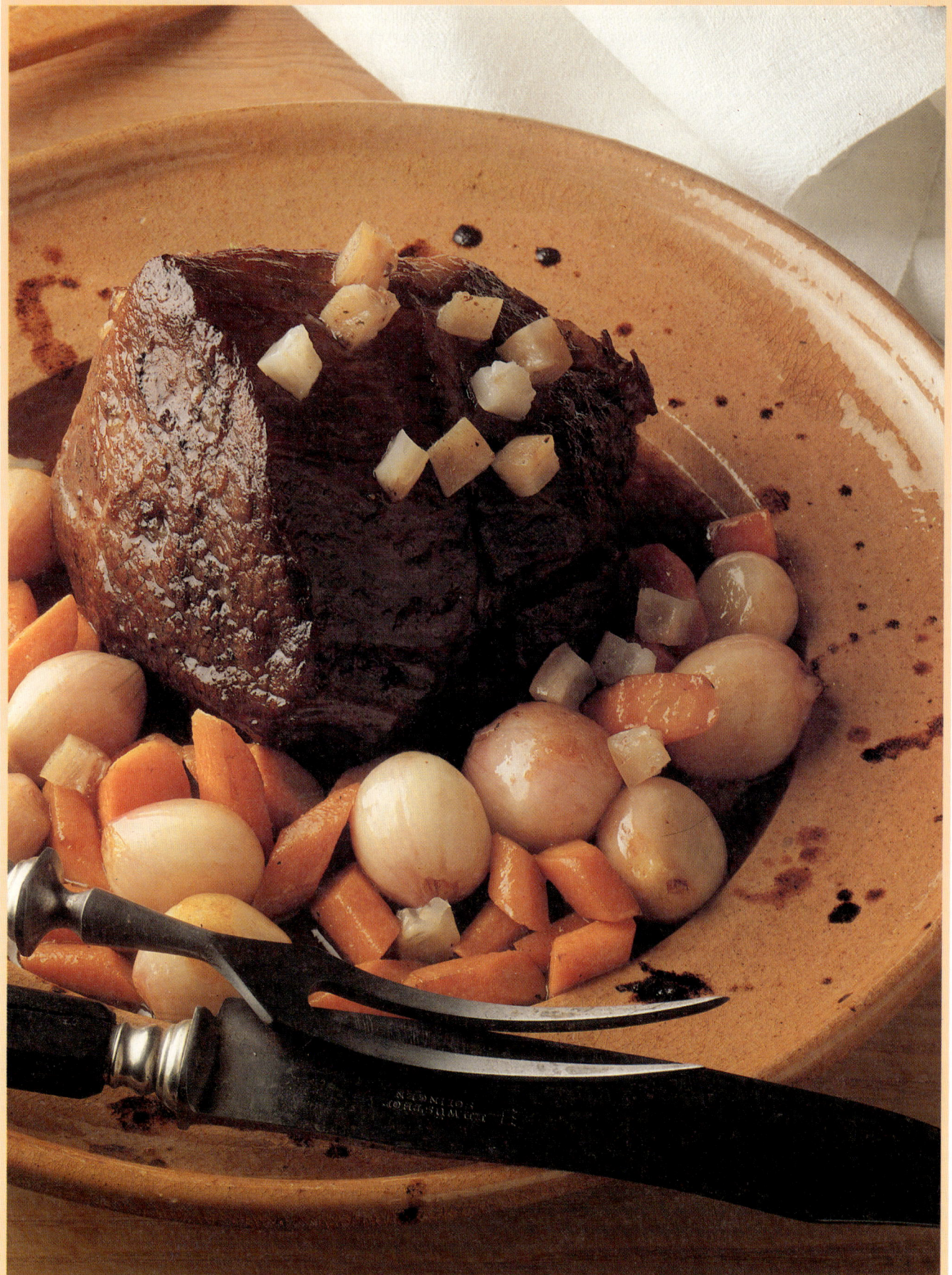

BEEF STROGANOFF

SERVES 4
Preparation and cooking time: 30 minutes
Kcal per serving: 355
P = 26g, F = 26g, C = 3g

1½ pounds filet of beef
3 tbsps sunflower oil
2 small onions
⅔ cup mushrooms
1 tbsp butter
3 tbsps white wine
1 pickle
½ cup sour cream
1 tsp English mustard
salt
freshly ground black pepper

1. Cut the beef into short, thick strips. Heat the oil in a skillet and fry the meat. The strips should remain pink in the middle. Remove the meat from the pan and keep warm.
2. Peel and chop the onions. Thinly slice the mushrooms.
3. Add the butter to the pan, and melt. Fry the onions until transparent. Add the mushrooms, and fry for 2–3 minutes. Add the wine.
4. Thinly slice the pickle, and add to the pan. Mix together the sour cream and mustard, add to the pan, bring to the boil, and allow to reduce a little. Return the meat to the pan, and heat through. Season to taste with salt and pepper.
Serving suggestions: small roast potatoes.
Recommended drinks: a dry white wine.

VIENNESE TAFELSPITZ

SERVES 4-6
Preparation and cooking time: 2–3 hours
Kcal per serving if serving 4: 350
P = 44g, F = 18g, C = 4g

2½ pounds top round of beef
1½ pounds beef bones
2 quarts water
salt
1 leek
1 carrot
½ head celery
1 onion
6 white peppercorns

1. Wash the meat and bones.
2. Bring the water to the boil in a large pan, season lightly with salt, and add the beef bones. Trim, wash, and slice the leek. Peel and slice the carrot. Trim and slice the celery. Peel the onion.
3. Add the beef, leek, carrot, celery, onion, and peppercorns to the pan and bring back to the boil. Cover the pan and lower the heat.
4. Simmer gently for 2–3 hours, skimming off the froth frequently. Transfer the beef to a warm serving dish and cut into finger-thick slices. Strain the cooking liquid and pour a little over the meat before serving.
Serving suggestions: horseradish sauce, roast, or boiled potatoes, spinach or leeks.
Recommended drinks: beer or medium red wine.

FRENCH MEATLOAF

SERVES 6
Preparation and cooking time: 1 hour
Kcal per serving: 255
P = 18g, F = 13g, C = 14g

2 tbsps butter
1 onion
6 ounces ham
2 potatoes, peeled and boiled
8 ounces lean ground beef
4 tbsps blanched almonds
2 thick slices white bread, crusts removed and soaked in water and squeezed dry
2 eggs, separated
pinch freshly grated nutmeg
1 tsp curry powder
4 tsps brandy
salt

1. Grease a loaf pan.
2. Peel the onion. Coarsely chop the ham, onion, and potatoes in a food processor. Mix the ham mixture, almonds, bread, egg yolks, nutmeg, curry powder, 1

Combine the ham, onion and potatoes in a food processor.

tbsp of the butter, and the brandy, and season with salt. Knead thoroughly.
3. Whisk the egg whites and fold into the mixture. Spoon into the loaf pan. Melt the remaining butter and brush over the surface. Bake at 475°F for about 30 minutes. Serve hot or cold.
Serving suggestion: salad.
Recommended drink: a hearty red wine.

INDIAN BEEF CURRY

SERVES 4
Preparation and cooking time: 1¼ hours
Marinate overnight
Kcal per serving: 370
P = 26g, F = 29g, C = 1g

1½ pounds topside of beef
2 tsps salt
2 tsps ground coriander (cilantro)
½ tsp ground turmeric
½ tsp ground cumin
1 tsp chili powder
½ tsp ground black pepper
1 tbsp chopped fresh root ginger
8 tbsps oil
1 tbsp milk
1 large onion
1–3 garlic cloves
1 cup water
pinch ground cinnamon
pinch ground cloves
1 tbsp chopped fresh coriander (cilantro) leaves

1. Cut the beef into cubes and place in a shallow dish.
2. Combine the salt, ground coriander, turmeric, cumin, chili powder, pepper, ginger, and half the oil. Add the milk and stir to make a smooth paste. Pour this over the beef cubes and toss to coat thoroughly. Set aside overnight to marinate.
3. Peel and slice the onion and garlic.
4. Heat the remaining oil, fry the onion and garlic until golden-brown. Add the beef, and fry for 8–10 minutes, stirring frequently, until brown. Stir in the water.
5. Cover and cook over a low heat for 45 minutes. Add more water if the sauce becomes too thick.
6. Season the curry with the cinnamon and cloves. Transfer to a serving dish and sprinkle with the coriander.
Serving suggestions: fluffy rice and a salad with yogurt dressing.
Recommended drink: a chilled beer.

THAI PORK AND SHRIMP

Nja Tdang

SERVES 4 ■

*Preparation and cooking
time: 30 minutes
Kcal per serving: 210
P = 25g, F = 11g, C = 3g*

3 tbsps dried Chinese
    mushrooms
1 onion
1 garlic clove
2 green chilies
3 tbsps vegetable oil
8 ounces ground pork
1 tbsp finely chopped root
    ginger
1¼ cups coconut milk
1 cup cooked shrimp, shelled
1 tbsp soy sauce
2 tbsps fish sauce
½ tsp sugar
salt
1 tbsp chopped coriander
    (cilantro) leaves

1. Rinse the mushrooms, place in a bowl, cover with hot water, and set aside to soak for about 10 minutes. Drain well and reserve the soaking liquid.
2. Peel and finely chop the onion and garlic. Seed the chilies. Heat the oil in a wok or skillet, and stir-fry the ground pork. Add the ginger, garlic, and onion, and stir-fry until the onion begins to color. Stir in the mushrooms and the chilies, and fry for a further 4 minutes.
3. Strain the mushroom soaking liquid through a fine sieve and combine with the coconut milk. Stir the liquid into the pork-and-onion mixture, and heat through.
4. Add the shrimp, and return the liquid to the boil. Add the soy sauce, fish sauce, sugar and, if necessary, season with a little salt. Serve garnished with chopped coriander (cilantro) leaves.
If canned coconut milk is not available, grate some fresh

Virtually all oriental dishes require garlic.

Wash the mushrooms and soak in hot water; they will swell considerably.

Stir-fry all the ingredients in a wok.

coconut or shred in a food processor. Add boiling water, allowing 2 cups for each 1 cup coconut. Set aside for 15 minutes before straining the liquid through cheesecloth. Shredded coconut may also be used.
Serving suggestion: rice.

HUNGARIAN GOULASH

SERVES 4 ■ ■

*Preparation and cooking
time: 1½ hours
Kcal per serving: 600
P = 23g, F = 54g, C = 6g*

2 onions
1½ pounds pork shoulder or
    neck
8 tbsps lard or pork fat
1 tsp sweet paprika
8 yellow or green bell
    peppers
1½ cups ripe tomatoes
salt

1. Peel and chop the onions. Rinse the pork and pat dry. Dice the pork. Melt the lard or fat in a large pot, and stir-fry the onions until transparent. Sprinkle with the paprika and add the pork. Cook over a low heat for 1 hour. If all the liquid evaporates, add ½ cup water.
2. Halve, seed, and wash the peppers, and cut into matchstick strips. Blanch, skin, and chop the tomatoes. Add the peppers and tomatoes to the casserole. Cover and cook over a low heat for a further 20 minutes. Season to taste with salt and serve.
Serving suggestions: mashed or boiled potatoes.
Recommended drink: a hearty red country wine.

FLORENTINE ROAST PORK

(photograph page 25)

SERVES 6–8 ■

*Preparation and cooking
time: 2½ hours
Kcal per serving if serving 6:
390
P = 36g, F = 24g, C = 6g*

3½ pounds boned loin of pork
1 garlic clove
1 tbsp fresh rosemary leaves
salt
freshly ground black pepper
4 sprigs fresh rosemary
4 potatoes

1. Rinse the meat and pat dry. Peel the garlic. Chop the rosemary leaves and garlic finely, and season to taste with salt and pepper. Rub the mixture into the pork. Arrange the rosemary sprigs on the meat and tie in place with trussing thread. Attach the pork to a spit with a pan for the juices underneath or place it in a roasting pan.
2. Peel and quarter the potatoes and arrange them in the spit pan or roasting pan. Sprinkle with salt.
3. Spit-roast the pork or roast in a preheated oven at 450°F for 2 hours, basting well with the cooking juices. Remove the pork from the spit or the roasting pan, cut the thread, and discard the rosemary sprigs. Carve the joint into slices and arrange on a serving dish with the roast potatoes.
Serving suggestion: broiled tomatoes.
Recommended drink: chianti or Italian red wine.

MIDDLE EASTERN LEG OF LAMB

SERVES 6 ■
Preparation and cooking time: 2–3 hours
Kcal per serving: 555
P = 35g, F = 36g, C = 23g

3½ pounds leg of lamb
3–4 garlic cloves
salt
freshly ground black pepper
3 tbsps olive oil
2 pounds potatoes
2 large onions
2 cups canned tomatoes
1 tsp chopped oregano
1–2 eggplant

Potatoes, tomatoes, onions, eggplant, and garlic are cooked with the lamb.

Pierce the flesh with a pointed knife and insert slivers of garlic into the slits.

Add the eggplant when the meat has cooked for 45 minutes.

1. Rinse the lamb and pat dry. Peel and thinly slice the garlic. Pierce the lamb in a number of places with a pointed knife and press slivers of garlic into the slits. Rub plenty of salt and pepper into the meat. Heat the oil in a large roasting pan and fry the lamb until browned all over. Arrange it in the roasting pan, fatty side down, and set aside.
2. Peel and thickly slice the potatoes. Peel the onions and slice the tomatoes. Arrange the potatoes, onions, and tomatoes around the meat, and season with salt and pepper. Sprinkle over the oregano.
3. Roast in a preheated oven at 350°F for 45 minutes.
4. Meanwhile, wash and slice the eggplant. Sprinkle the slices with salt and set aside for 30 minutes to drain. Pat dry and arrange them around the meat in the roasting pan.
5. Return the roasting pan to the oven for a further 1¼ hours, basting the lamb with the cooking juices from time to time, and turning the joint over once. Turn the vegetables once during cooking to ensure that they cook evenly. Spoon out any excess fat.

If the vegetables become too dry, a little water may be added.
6. Carve the leg of lamb into slices and arrange on a serving dish with the vegetables.
Serving suggestion: mixed salad.
Recommended drink: a hearty red wine.

TURKISH LAMB MEATBALLS WITH YOGURT

SERVES 4 ■
Preparation and cooking time: 20 minutes
Kcal per serving: 545
P = 31g, F = 42g, C = 10g

3 garlic cloves
1½ pounds boneless lamb, diced
salt
freshly ground black pepper
2–3 tbsps vegetable oil
2 tsps cornstarch
1¼ cup Greek yogurt
pinch sweet paprika (optional)
8 fresh mint sprigs

1. Peel the garlic, mix with the lamb, and chop finely in a food processor. Season to taste with salt and pepper. Shape a number of small meatballs with wet hands, and brush them with oil.
2. Cook the meatballs under a preheated broiler until crisp and brown all over. Alternatively, heat the oil in a skillet, and fry the meatballs until crisp and brown all over. Transfer to a warmed serving dish and keep warm.
3. Stir the cornstarch into the yogurt in a small saucepan. Gently heat through, stirring constantly. Season with salt.
4. Pour the yogurt over the meatballs and sprinkle with pepper or paprika, if liked, and garnish with the mint.
Serving suggestion: tomato salad.

LAMB NOISETTES WITH TARRAGON

Noisettes d'agneau à l'estragon

SERVES 4 ■
Preparation and cooking time: 20 minutes
Marinate for 12 hours
Kcal per serving: 555
P = 25g, F = 47g, C = 2g

8 x lamb noisettes (3 ounces each)
3 tbsps vegetable oil
2 tbsp chopped tarragon
salt
freshly ground black pepper
1 tbsp butter

FOR THE SAUCE:
2 shallots
½ cup white wine
1 tbsp wine vinegar
2 tarragon sprigs
4 tbsps butter, diced

1. Flatten the noisettes to make round steaks. Arrange in a shallow dish. Mix together the oil and tarragon, pour over the lamb, and marinate for 12 hours.
2. Drain the noisettes and dry-fry until browned. Turn and season to taste. Add the butter, and fry each side for 3 minutes. Remove from the pan and keep warm.
3. Peel and finely chop the shallots. Add to the wine vinegar and add 1 tarragon sprig. Boil for 5 minutes. Strain.
4. Discard the fat from the roasting pan. Add the wine mixture and place over a low heat, scraping the bottom of the pan to deglaze. Chop the remaining tarragon, and add to the sauce. Remove from the heat and stir in the butter, 1 piece at a time. Arrange the lamb on a warm serving dish and pour the sauce over it.
Serving suggestion: Lyonnaise potatoes.
Recommended drink: a fruity white wine.

DEEP-FRIED MEATBALLS
CHINESE STYLE

DEEP-FRIED MEATBALLS CHINESE STYLE

SERVES 4
Preparation and cooking time: 30 minutes
Kcal per serving: 255
P = 29g, F = 13g, C = 6g

1½ pounds boned pork shoulder
½ tsp salt
1 tsp monosodium glutamate (optional)
1 tsp rice wine or medium sherry
1 tbsp sesame oil
½ tsp minced fresh root ginger
2 tsps chopped green onions (scallions)
1 egg, lightly beaten
2 tbsps cornstarch
1 tbsp water
oil for deep-frying

1. Finely chop the pork. Mix together the pork, salt, monosodium glutamate (if using), rice wine or sherry, sesame oil, ginger, onions, egg, 2 tsps of the cornstarch and the water. Knead thoroughly to make a smooth mixture.
2. Shape the mixture into small meatballs, and dip them in the remaining cornstarch.
3. Heat the oil in a wok or skillet, and stir-fry the meatballs for about 5 minutes until they are golden-brown all over. Drain and serve immediately.
The pork for these meatballs should be ground not by the butcher but at home in a food processor. In this way the meat fibers are not so badly damaged.
Serving suggestions: rice and Chinese (Nappa) cabbage.
Recommended drinks: beer, a dry rosé wine or China tea.

CANTONESE FONDUE

(photograph page 40)

SERVES 10
Preparation and cooking time: 2 hours
Kcal per serving: 315
P = 31g, F = 17g, C = 12g

8 ounces beef sirloin
8 ounces lamb filet
8 ounces pork filet
5½ ounces pig's liver or pig's kidneys
8 ounces fish fillet
10 cubes tofu
1 small Chinese (Nappa) cabbage
10 thin green onions (scallions)
4 ounces cellophane noodles, soaked
1 cup raw shrimp, shelled

FOR THE DIP:
12 tbsps soy sauce
1 tsp ground ginger
2 tbsps minced shallots
6 tbsps soya oil
2 tbsps minced parsley

FOR THE BROTH:
1½ quarts chicken broth
4 slices fresh root ginger
salt
freshly ground white pepper

1. Place the beef, lamb, and pork in the freezer until partially frozen. Cut into wafer-thin slices. Spread them out on a large dish. Blanch the liver or kidneys in boiling water for 2 minutes and then plunge straight into cold water. Thinly slice. Thinly slice the fish fillet. Soak the tofu in cold water for 1 minute, drain, and cut in quarters. Wash and shred the cabbage. Trim and wash the green onions. Strain the noodles. Arrange all the ingredients attractively on dishes.
2. To make the dip, mix together all the ingredients in a small pan, and bring to the boil. Divide the dip between 10 small bowls.

Cut the meat into wafer-thin slices. Cut the fish into thicker slices.

Cellophane noodles, green onions (scallions), tofu, ginger, and Chinese (Nappa) cabbage are classic ingredients in Chinese cooking.

3. To prepare the broth, place the chicken broth and root ginger in an earthenware fondue pan. Season to taste with salt and pepper, and bring to the boil. Transfer the fondue pan to the heat.
4. Arrange all the prepared ingredients around the fondue and place a soup bowl and a dish of the dip in front of each guest.
5. Each guest chooses their ingredients, holding them with a fondue fork or chopsticks. They are then dipped first into the boiling broth until cooked, and then the dip. Finally, the broth is drunk as a soup from the bowls.
Serving suggestion: shrimp crackers.
Recommended drinks: China tea or rice wine.

MIXED GRILL

SERVES 4
Preparation and cooking time: 30 minutes
Marinate for 2 hours
Kcal per serving: 605
P = 33g, F = 52g, C = 0g

4 small slices beef filet
4 lamb cutlets
1–2 tbsps oil
4 small veal filet slices
4 small pork sausages or 4 small slices calf's liver
4 thin slices bacon
salt
freshly ground black pepper

FOR THE MARINADE:
1 garlic clove
5 tbsps oil
½ tsp black peppercorns, crushed

1. First make the marinade. Peel and crush the garlic. Mix together the oil, garlic, and crushed peppercorns. Brush the marinade over the beef filet slices and the lamb cutlets, and set aside in the refrigerator for 2 hours. Turn the meat over occasionally.
2. Brush the broiler pan with a little oil and pre-heat.
3. Brush some of the marinade over the veal and liver, if using. Arrange the meat, sausages, or liver and bacon side-by-side on the broiler pan, and broil on both sides until golden-brown. After turning, season with salt and pepper. Brush with some of the marinade from time to time. The meat should be tender when pressed, and all but the sausages should still be pink in the center.
4. Arrange the cooked meats on a wooden platter or a large serving dish.
Serving suggestions: foil-wrapped baked potatoes, broiled tomatoes, and herb butter.
Recommended drink: a hearty red wine.

Cooking for Special Occasions

When lovers of fine food are in the mood for meat, then classical haute cuisine recipes will be on the menu. Inevitably, tender pieces of beef, veal, and lamb will be most in demand, and yet it could just as easily be a pork sparerib roast that has absorbed the delicate flavors of a spicy white wine marinade. Many people prefer not to feast on large roasts or huge steaks – there are, after all, other things to enjoy apart from meat – but the meat course is often the highlight of a special occasion meal. Moreover, the cook will invariably be judged by his or her ability to create something special from top-quality ingredients. This chapter offers a selection of the best classical meat recipes.

Sirloin Steaks with Anchovy Cream
(recipe page 58)

MUSTARD BEEF

SERVES 6 ■ ■ ■
Preparation and cooking time: 1½ hours
Marinate for 2 days
Kcal per serving: 500
P = 31g, F = 34g, C = 1g

3 pounds forerib of beef
1 garlic clove
1 small hot chili pepper
2 cups red wine
1 bayleaf
1 tbsp rosemary leaves
salt
freshly ground black pepper
2 tbsps olive oil
2 tbsps Dijon mustard

1. Rinse the meat and pat dry. Place in a dish.
2. Peel and crush the garlic. Seed and wash the chili. Place the wine, garlic, chili, bayleaf, and rosemary in a small pan, and season with pepper. Bring to the boil, remove from the heat, and set aside to cool.
3. When the mixture is cool, pour it over the meat and set aside in the refrigerator for 36 hours, turning the meat two or three times each day.

Boil the red wine and spices and then leave to cool.

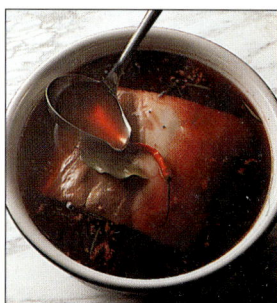
Cover the meat with the cold marinade and leave to stand in the refrigerator for 1½ days.

5. Return the beef to the oven and roast for 40 minutes, basting frequently, until it is pink. Just before it is ready, cover with aluminum foil.
6. Before carving, turn off the oven and leave the beef to stand for 3–4 minutes, so that all the juice does not run out when it is cut.
7. Dilute the meat juices with the marinade, bring to the boil, and allow to reduce. Serve the gravy separately.
Serving suggestions: gratin dauphinois and a mixed salad.
Recommended drink: a good Burgundy wine.

> **TIP**
>
> *Forerib generally refers to ribs 6 to 12 and this cut should ideally be served rare to medium.*
> *Use a meat thermometer to check whether the meat is cooked according to your requirements.*

4. Remove the beef from the marinade, pat dry, and brush with oil. Reserve the marinade. Place the beef in a roasting pan and brown in a preheated oven at 475°F. Sprinkle with salt and coat with the mustard.

ENTRECÔTE WITH CHERVIL SAUCE

SERVES 2 ■ ■
Preparation and cooking time: 30–35 minutes
Kcal per serving: 420
P = 24g, F = 35g, C = 2g

1 x 10 ounce entrecôte steak
salt
freshly ground black pepper
1 shallot
3 tbsps butter
2 tsps chopped fresh chervil
2 small zucchini
½ tsp paprika
5 tbsps heavy cream
pinch cayenne pepper

1. Remove the steak from the refrigerator 30 minutes before it is required. Pat dry and score the rind a number of times so that it does not contract when cooked. Rub salt into the meat, sprinkle generously with pepper, cover, and leave to stand at room temperature.
2. Meanwhile, peel and chop the shallot. Melt 1 tbsp of the butter in a skillet, and gently fry the shallot and half the chervil. Remove from the heat and set aside.
3. Melt the remaining butter in another pan, and fry the steak for 6–7 minutes on each side. Make sure that it remains pink in the center. For a rare steak, 3–4 minutes on each side is sufficient. Once the steak has been turned, sprinkle with salt. Wrap the steak in aluminum foil when cooked.
4. Wash, peel, and chop the zucchini. Place them in the meat juices over a high heat. Sprinkle over the paprika and stir-fry until very little of the liquid remains.
5. Add the shallot mixture and the cream to the pan and boil, stirring constantly, until it reaches a thick and creamy consistency. Season with salt and cayenne pepper.

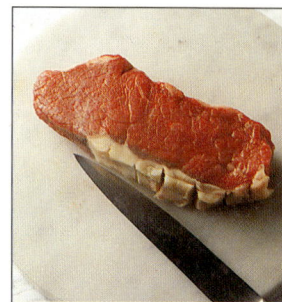
Make a number of cuts in the fatty edge of the steak so that it retains its shape when fried.

Wrap the entrecôte in aluminum foil while preparing the sauce.

6. Cut the steak across the grain into ½-inch slices. Pour the sauce onto warmed plates and arrange the meat slices on top. Sprinkle with the remaining chervil.
Serving suggestions: sliced roast potatoes and mixed vegetables.
Recommended drink: a medium red wine.

> **TIP**
>
> *Cook the zucchini at the highest heat possible to prevent the liquid from escaping.*

BEEF FILETS WITH CEPS AND RED WINE SAUCE

SERVES 4 ■ ■
Preparation and cooking time: 40 minutes
Kcal per serving: 355
P = 36g, F = 18g, C = 2g

3 shallots or 1 onion
4 tbsps butter
2 tbsps dried ceps (porcini)
1 cup red wine
3 tbsps concentrated beef broth
4 x 6 ounce beef filets
salt
freshly ground black pepper
1 tsp minced parsley

1. Peel and finely chop the shallots or onion. Melt 1 tbsp of the butter, and stir-fry the shallots for 5 minutes. Remove from the heat and set aside.
2. Place the ceps in a bowl, cover with water, and set aside to soak.
3. Place half the shallots and ¾ cup of the wine in a small pan. Bring to the boil and allow to reduce by half.

> ### TIP
> *If using fresh ceps, do not add them to the sauce, but fry them quickly in butter just before serving.*

4. Drain the ceps and add to the reduced wine. Add the remaining wine and the broth, bring to the boil, and allow to reduce by half.
5. Melt 1 tbsp of the remaining butter, and fry the beef until rare or medium, according to taste. Season with salt and pepper and arrange on a warm serving dish. Add the reserved shallots.

Combine half the cooked shallots with ¾ cup red wine and allow to reduce by half.

Add the soaked ceps to the concentrated beef broth and reduce by half again.

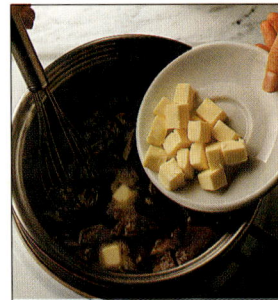
Beat the diced butter into the red wine sauce.

6. Dice the remaining butter. Remove the sauce from the heat and allow to cool slightly. Beat in the butter a few pieces at a time. Continue to beat until the sauce is light and creamy. Season the beef filets again with salt and pepper, if necessary, pour over the sauce and sprinkle with parsley.
Serving suggestions: cream potatoes and fresh green vegetables.
Recommended drink: a good full-bodied red wine.

FILLET OF BEEF IN SHERRY VINEGAR

SERVES 4 ■ ■
Preparation and cooking time: 50 minutes
Kcal per serving: 265
P = 29g, F = 16g, C = 3g

3 tbsps butter
1½ pounds filet of beef
2 tbsps sherry vinegar
2 kiwi fruits
½ cup veal broth or a thin broth
1 garlic clove
1 tbsp tomato paste
pinch sugar
pinch cayenne pepper
salt
freshly ground black pepper

1. Melt 1 tbsp of the butter, and fry the beef until browned on all sides. Add the sherry vinegar and scrape the base of the pan with a spatula to deglaze. Partially cover and cook for a further 10 minutes. Remove the filet from the skillet and keep warm.
2. Peel the kiwi fruits. Dice 1 and slice the other. Purée the diced kiwi fruit and the broth in a blender.
3. Peel and crush the garlic clove. Add the garlic to the sherry vinegar mixture, and stir in the kiwi fruit mixture, tomato paste, sugar, and cayenne pepper over a low heat. Season with salt and pepper and remove the pan from the heat.
4. Dice the remaining butter and stir into the sauce. Pour onto warmed plates.
5. Cut the filet into slices and arrange on the sauce. Garnish with kiwi fruit slices.
Serving suggestions: rice and leaf spinach.
Recommended drink: a red or white country wine.

SIRLOIN STEAKS WITH ANCHOVY CREAM

(photograph page 54)

SERVES 4 ■ ■
Preparation and cooking time: 15–20 minutes
Kcal per serving: 390
P = 31g, F = 26g, C = 1g

1 tbsp butter
4 x 6 ounce sirloin steaks

FOR THE SAUCE:
½ cup ruby port
3 anchovy fillets
4 tbsps heavy cream
1 garlic clove
4 tbsps butter
salt
freshly ground black pepper
1 tbsp chopped fresh basil

FOR THE GARNISH:
4 anchovy fillets
4 black olives

1. Melt the butter, and fry the steaks for 2–3 minutes on each side until rare or medium, according to taste. Remove from the pan and keep warm.
2. Add the port to the pan, bring to the boil, and allow to reduce by half.
3. Drain the anchovy fillets and pat dry. Chop finely and mash or purée in a blender.
4. Crush the garlic clove and combine with the anchovy purée, cream, and reduced port. Allow to reduce again until the sauce is light and creamy.
5. Lower the heat. Dice the butter, and stir into the sauce. Season to taste with salt and pepper, and stir in the basil. Remember that anchovies are very salty.
6. Arrange the steaks on warmed plates, pour the sauce over them and garnish each with an anchovy and an olive.
Serving suggestion: zucchini.

ROLLED BREAST OF VEAL

SERVES 3 ■ ■

Preparation and cooking time: 45–50 minutes
Kcal per serving: 385
P = 39g, F = 22g, C = 1g

½ cup mushrooms
1½ pounds boned breast of veal
2 garlic cloves
3 tbsps butter
2 tbsps finely chopped fresh mixed herbs
salt
freshly ground black pepper
1 cup white wine
½ cup broth

1. Chop the mushrooms. Rinse the breast of veal, pat dry, and lay out on the work top.
2. Crush the garlic. Melt 1 tbsp of the butter, and gently fry the garlic, herbs, and mushrooms.
3. Spread the mixture over the veal, and season to taste with salt and pepper. Roll up the veal and secure with trussing thread.
4. Melt the remaining butter in a large pot, and fry the veal until browned all over. Season again with salt and pepper.
5. Roast the veal in a pre-heated oven at 350–400°F for 25–30 minutes. From time to time add a little wine.
6. Remove the veal from the pot, place on a large serving platter and remove the trussing thread. Keep warm. Add the broth to the cooking juices, set over a medium heat and allow to reduce.
7. Remove the thread and carve the rolled veal at the table. Pour a little gravy over it.
Serving suggestions: potato pancakes and fresh green vegetables.
Recommended drink: a red country wine.

Gently fry the mushrooms, crushed garlic, and chopped herbs in butter.

Spread the mixture over the breast of veal.

Roll up the veal, starting at the narrow end. Ensure that the filling does not squeeze out at the sides.

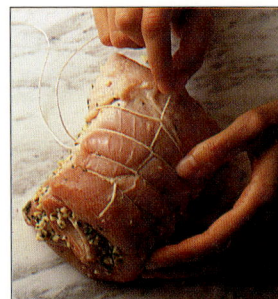

Secure the veal roll with trussing thread.

VEAL SCALLOPS WITH SWEET-AND-SOUR SAUCE

SERVES 4 ■ ■

Preparation and cooking time: 45 minutes
Kcal per serving: 170
P = 21g, F = 4g, C = 7g

1 carrot
1 onion
1 pound veal bones, crushed
½ bayleaf
1 clove
4 x 4 ounces thin veal scallops
1 tbsp butter
salt
freshly ground black pepper
1 tbsp sugar
3 tbsps lemon juice
1 garlic clove
1 tsp grated lemon rind
1 tbsp tomato paste
1 tsp cornstarch
2 tsps soy sauce
2 tbsps white wine or sherry
pinch cayenne pepper

1. Peel and dice the carrot. Peel and coarsely chop the onion. Place the bones in a pan with 1 cup water, the carrot, onion, bayleaf, and clove, bring to the boil, and simmer for 20 minutes. Strain, and return to the pan. Bring to the boil and reduce to 6 tbsps.
2. Melt the butter, and fry the veal until browned on both sides. Remove from the pan, season with salt and pepper, and keep warm.
3. Place the sugar in a small pan and heat gently until it becomes runny. Stir well and allow to caramelize. Add 1 tbsp broth, followed by 1 tbsp lemon juice.
4. Add the meat juices to the remaining broth and heat through. Peel and crush the garlic. Add to the broth together with the caramel, lemon rind, tomato paste and remaining lemon juice. Season with salt and pepper, and bring to the boil.

The veal escalopes should be very thin. If necessary, flatten with a steak hammer.

5. Stir together the cornstarch, soy sauce, and white wine or sherry and add to the sweet-and-sour sauce. Continue to boil until the sauce starts to thicken. Season with cayenne pepper, and pour the sauce over the meat.
Serving suggestions: rice, broccoli, or snowpeas.
Recommended drink: rosé wine.

> ### TIP
> *The veal scallops should be very thin. If necessary, place them in a plastic bag and flatten them with a steak hammer. As an alternative, replace the veal with thinly sliced turkey breast.*

VEAL IN A ROASTING BAG

SERVES 4 ■■
Preparation and cooking time: 50 minutes
Kcal per serving: 280
P = 33g, F = 15g, C = 3g

1½ pounds shoulder of veal
salt
freshly ground black pepper
2 slices bacon, rinded
10 sage leaves
2 carrots
1 stick celery
pinch ground mace
1 small garlic clove, peeled
1 onion, studded with 1 clove
1 bayleaf
4 tbsps veal broth
1 tbsp tomato paste
1 tbsp butter

1. Rinse the veal and pat dry. Make deep cuts in the veal at ½–¾-inch intervals. Sprinkle pepper between the slices and then tuck a small piece of bacon and a small sage leaf (or half a leaf) in the cuts. Tie the joint together lengthwise with trussing thread.
2. Peel and chop the carrots. Trim and chop the celery.
3. Cut a length of roasting bag 1½ times the length of the joint and seal one end.
4. Rub the mace and salt into the meat, place it in the bag, and add the garlic, onion, bayleaf, carrot, and celery. Seal the bag and pierce a number of holes in it with a pointed knife.
5. Place the roasting bag on a baking sheet, and cook the veal in a preheated oven at 425°F for 35 minutes.
6. Remove the bag from the oven and cut open the top. Pour the meat juices into a small pan. Turn off the oven and place the meat inside to keep warm.
7. Add the broth to the meat juices, bring to the boil, and allow to reduce by a half. Add the tomato paste, season with salt and pepper,

Make deep cuts in the top of the joint and place a little bacon and sage between the slices.

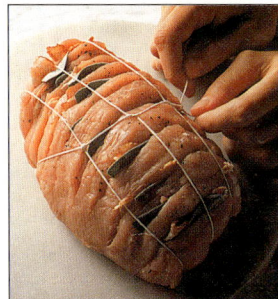
Tie the veal joint together with trussing thread.

Place the meat and vegetables inside the roasting bag and seal the ends tightly.

and remove from the heat. Dice the butter and stir into the gravy one piece at a time. Carve the veal and arrange on a warm serving platter and hand the gravy separately.
Serving suggestions: risotto or noodles.
Recommended drink: chianti Classico.

KNUCKLE OF VEAL IN ORANGE SAUCE

(photograph page 15)

SERVES 4 ■■
Preparation and cooking time: 1 hour 50 minutes
Marinate overnight
Kcal per serving: 385
P = 54g, F = 12g, C = 11g

1 orange
2 garlic cloves
1 carrot
2 medium onions
3 tbsps olive oil
2 tbsps lemon juice
½ cup orange juice
3-4 allspice berries
4 slices knuckle of veal
   (about 2½ pounds)
salt
freshly ground black pepper
1 bayleaf
½ cup white wine
½ meat broth cube
pinch cayenne pepper
1 tbsp minced parsley

1. Wash the orange, peel thinly, and chop the rind finely. Peel and crush the garlic. Peel and chop the carrot and onions.
2. Mix together 2 tbsps of the olive oil, the lemon juice, orange juice, garlic, carrot, onion, orange rind, and allspice berries.
3. Rinse the veal slices and pat dry. Sprinkle generously with pepper and then dip them in the orange marinade. Place them in a shallow dish and pour the remaining marinade over them. Add the bayleaf and set aside in the refrigerator overnight.
4. Remove the veal from the marinade, scraping off the bits with a spatula. Reserve the marinade. Heat the remaining olive oil in a flameproof casserole, and fry the veal until browned on all sides. Season with salt and pepper.

Wash the orange well, peel it thinly, and chop the rind finely.

Sprinkle the veal slices with pepper, cover with the marinade, and refrigerate overnight.

Remove the veal from the marinade, scraping it with a spatula.

5. Add the reserved marinade, cover, and cook gently for 1½ hours, gradually adding the wine during the cooking time. Transfer the veal to a warm serving dish.
6. Stir the broth cube into the sauce, and season with salt and cayenne pepper. Remove and discard the bayleaf. Pour the sauce over the veal and serve garnished with the minced parsley.
Serving suggestions: fried zucchini and rice.

PORK SPARERIB IN WHITE WINE

SERVES 4 ■
Preparation and cooking time: 3 hours 25 minutes
Marinate for 1–2
Kcal per serving: 645
P = 35g, F = 37g, C = 10g

1½ pounds lean pork
*   spareribs*
2 large onions
1 clove
1 carrot
1 small leek
2 tbsps celery
1 bayleaf
1 thyme sprig
1 rosemary sprig
1 sage sprig
1 marjoram sprig
1 basil sprig
1 bottle white wine
2 tbsps butter
salt
freshly ground black pepper
6 tbsps heavy cream
⅔ cup mushrooms

1. Place the pork in a deep dish. Peel 1 onion, stud with the clove, and add to the dish. Peel and chop the carrot. Trim, wash, and chop the leek and celery. Peel and chop the remaining onion.
2. Add the carrot, leek, celery, chopped onion, bayleaf, thyme, rosemary, sage, marjoram, and basil to the dish. Pour over sufficient wine just to cover the pork. Set aside for 1–2 days to marinate, turning the meat each day.
3. Remove the pork from the marinade. Strain the marinade through a sieve into a pan, bring to the boil, and skim off any froth. Reserve the vegetables.
4. Pat the pork dry. Heat half the butter in a roasting pan and brown the pork all over. Remove from the pan and stir the reserved vegetables into the pan juices.
5. Season the pork with salt and pepper and then return it to the roasting pan. Add half the marinade and cook

in a preheated oven at its lowest setting (175°F) for 3 hours. Add a little more marinade from time to time.
6. Transfer the pork to a large dish and cover with foil. Switch off the oven and leave the meat to rest for 10 minutes.
7. Meanwhile, strain the sauce into a skillet, bring to the boil and allow to reduce slightly. Stir in the cream, bring to the boil, again and season with salt and pepper, if necessary.
8. Wipe and slice the mushrooms. Melt the remaining butter, and gently fry the mushrooms.
9. Cut the meat into ½-inch slices and arrange on a serving dish. Top with the mushrooms. Serve the sauce separately.
Serving suggestion: mashed potato or green noodles.
Recommended drink: Zinfandel.

> **TIP**
>
> *The special flavor of this pork derives from the wine marinade and the herbs and vegetables. For this reason, a lengthy period of marinating is essential, even as long as 5 days.*

PORK STEAKS WITH AVOCADO SAUCE

SERVES 4 ■ ■
Preparation and cooking time: 40 minutes
Kcal per serving: 725
P = 31g, F = 66g, C = 2g

2 ripe avocados
2 tbsps lemon juice
4 x 6 ounce pork steaks
salt
freshly ground black pepper
4 tbsps butter
1 cup chicken broth
4 tbsps heavy cream
2 tsps curry powder
pinch cayenne pepper

1. Peel and pit the avocado pears. Brush the flesh of 1 avocado with lemon juice. Purée the other with a hand-held mixer or mash with a fork.

The avocado can be puréed with a hand-held blender.

2. Sprinkle the steaks with pepper. Melt the butter, and fry the pork until golden. Remove from the pan. Stir the broth into the meat juices and bring to the boil.
3. Combine the avocado purée and cream. Add the mixture to the broth, and season with curry powder, salt, and cayenne. Warm through but do not boil.
4. Warm the steaks in the sauce for 1–2 minutes. Slice the peeled avocado and arrange on the steaks.
Serving suggestion: rice.
Recommended drink: a red wine.

PORK CHOPS WITH SOUR CREAM SAUCE

SERVES 4 ■ ■
Preparation and cooking time: 35–40 minutes
Kcal per serving: 640
P = 34g, F = 52g, C = 8g

2 tbsps butter
1 tbsp capers
4 pork chops (about 8
*   ounces each)*
salt
freshly ground white pepper
4 tbsps chopped onions
2 tbsps white wine vinegar
1 tbsp clear honey
1 cup sour cream
1 tbsp chopped pickles
2 tsps chopped fresh tarragon
2 tsps strong mustard
1 tsp wholegrain mustard

1. Rinse the capers in cold water.
2. Melt the butter, and fry the chops until golden-brown on both sides. Season with salt and pepper, partially cover, and cook for 10–12 minutes. Remove from the pan and keep warm.
3. Pour off any excess fat. Add the onions to the pan, and gently fry for 2–3 minutes. Stir in the vinegar and honey.
4. Stir in the cream, bring to the boil, and season with salt and pepper. Add the pickles, half the tarragon, the strong mustard, and the wholegrain mustard. Mix thoroughly. Do not allow to boil.
5. Arrange the chops on a warmed serving dish and pour the sauce over them. Garnish with the remaining tarragon and the rinsed capers.
Serving suggestion: noodles, mashed potato, or rice.
Recommended drink: beer or a red wine.

HERBED RACK OF LAMB

SERVES 4 ■ ■

Preparation and cooking time: 50 minutes
Kcal per serving: 995
P = 37g, F = 88g, C = 6g

3 pounds lamb ribs
4 tbsps butter
salt
freshly ground black pepper
2 heads of garlic
1 carrot
1 tomato
1 cup Marsala or sherry
5 tbsps minced parsley
2 tbsps minced mixed fresh
   herbs
2 tbsps butter

Roast the halved garlic bulbs, carrot, and tomato with the lamb.

1. Rinse the lamb and pat dry. Melt half the butter in a flameproof oven dish, and brown the lamb in a preheated oven at 400°F, turning from time to time. Season with salt and pepper. Cut the garlic bulbs in half and place, face downward, in the bottom of the casserole. Peel the carrot. Add the carrot, and tomato to the casserole, cover and cook for a further 5 minutes.

TIP

Ask your butcher to chine the lamb to make carving a little easier. For really special occasions, use a whole loin of lamb (6 pounds is sufficient for 8 people).

2. Partially uncover the casserole and cook the meat for a further 10 minutes, gradually adding the Marsala during the cooking time.
3. Switch off the oven and leave the lamb to rest for 5 minutes.

Scoop the garlic cloves out of the bulb with a teaspoon.

4. Meanwhile, remove the garlic bulbs and scoop out the flesh with a teaspoon. Mix the garlic, parsley, and mixed herbs. Melt the remaining butter in a skillet, and gently fry the garlic-and-herb mixture for 5–6 minutes.
5. Transfer the lamb to a warm serving dish and coat the outer surface with a smooth layer of the herb mixture. Carve it at the table.
Serving suggestions: Lyonnaise potatoes and broccoli.
Recommended drink: rosé or a medium red wine.

LEG OF LAMB WITH ROSEMARY

(photograph page 19)

SERVES 3–4 ■ ■

Preparation and cooking time: 1¼ hours
Kcal per serving if serving 4: 790
P = 46g, F = 61g, C = 5g

3 pound leg of lamb
2–3 tbsps rosemary leaves
salt
freshly ground black pepper
6 tbsps butter
2 carrots
2 tomatoes
1 celery sprig
2 garlic cloves
1 bayleaf
1 cup white wine

1. Ask your butcher to remove the layer of fat from the leg of lamb. It may also be necessary to ask him to shorten the bones so that it fits into the roasting pan, but ask to keep the bones.
2. Wash the lamb and pat dry. Pierce a series of holes about ¾–1 inch deep with a larding needle. Insert a rosemary leaf into each hole. Season with salt and pepper.
3. Melt 2 tbsps of the butter in a roasting pan, add the lamb and any bones, baste with the melted butter, and roast in a preheated oven at 350°F.
4. Peel the carrots and cut in half lengthwise. Halve the tomatoes. Add the carrots, tomatoes, celery sprig, unpeeled garlic cloves, and bayleaf to the roasting pan.
5. Cover the meat with foil and roast for 45–50 minutes, gradually adding the wine during the cooking.
6. Switch off the oven. Transfer the lamb to a warmed platter and return to the oven to rest for a further 8 minutes.

Pierce holes in the lamb and stud with rosemary leaves.

Carve the meat into ½-inch slices.

7. Strain the meat juices into a small pan. Add 3–4 tbsps water to the roasting pan, bring to the boil, and pour into the pan. Set over a low heat. Dice the remaining butter, and beat into the cooking juices. Warm through, beating constantly, but do not boil. Season well and pour into a warmed gravy-boat.
8. Serve the carrots with the lamb, if liked, but discard the bayleaf, and garlic cloves.
9. Carve the meat at the table. First remove the upper and lower 'eye' from the bone. Place the roast across the carving board, and cut diagonal slices. The flesh should still be pink.
Serving suggestion: roast potatoes.
Recommended drink: a full-bodied red wine.

Wholefood Recipes

Meat normally occupies only a small place in wholefood recipe books, but these splendid recipes by Doris Katharina Hessler for beef, veal, lamb, and other meats go some way towards redressing the balance. Naturally, all the ingredients are fresh and require very short cooking times. Delicious vegetables, such as mushrooms, sweetcorn, and rice are combined to create healthy and tasty dishes. Of course, cereal grains, sprouts, pulses, and nuts accompany the meat, not to mention a range of aromatics, herbs, and spices – each used sparingly but with an important part to play in enhancing the meat's flavor. Inevitably the outcome will be not only wholesome and natural, but imaginative and unusual.

Loin of Lamb with Pistou au Gratin (recipe page 78)

BEEF FILET IN GORGONZOLA SAUCE

SERVES 4
*Preparation and cooking
time: 30 minutes
Kcal per serving: 595
P = 34g, F = 48g, C = 2g*

*1¾ cups home-made beef
   broth
1 cup heavy cream
4 tbsps butter
3 tbsps medium sherry
4 tsps sherry vinegar
1½ pounds filet of beef
salt
freshly ground white pepper
3 tbsps grapeseed oil
5–7 ounces Gorgonzola
   cheese
2 tbsps whipped cream*

1. Place the broth, heavy
cream, butter, sherry, and
vinegar in a pan. Bring to the
boil over a medium heat,
and allow to reduce by a
third.
2. Season the beef with salt
and pepper. Heat the oil in a
ovenproof pot, and brown
the beef all over. Transfer the
casserole to a preheated
oven and cook at 400°F for
10 minutes. Remove the
beef, wrap in foil, and leave
to rest for 10 minutes.
3. Dice the Gorgonzola
cheese, and add to the
reduced sauce. Purée with a
hand blender and then rub
through a sieve. Return to
the pan, bring to the boil,
and add the whipped cream.
4. Cut the beef into slices
and arrange on a serving
platter. Hand the sauce separately.
Serving suggestions: whole-
wheat noodles, broccoli, or
leaf spinach.
Recommended   drink: a
hearty white wine.

Brown the beef on all sides.

When cooked, wrap the filet in
foil for 10 minutes.

Purée the sauce and diced
Gorgonzola with a hand blender
and rub it through a sieve.

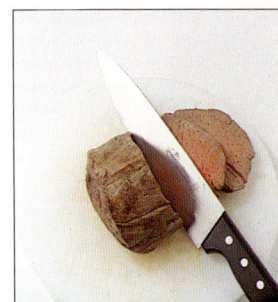
Cut the filet into slices with a
carving knife. Hand the sauce
separately.

BEEF FILETS ON A BED OF CREAMY VEGETABLES IN RED WINE AND MADEIRA SAUCE

SERVES 4
*Preparation and cooking
time: 50 minutes
Kcal per serving: 785
P = 22g, F = 57g, C = 18g*

*4 beef fillets (about 4 ounces)
salt
freshly ground white pepper
2 tbsps oil*

**FOR THE CREAMY
VEGETABLES:**
*4 ounces carrots
1 kohlrabi
4 sticks celery
2 leeks
1 tbsp butter or margarine
salt
freshly ground white pepper
⅔ cup heavy cream
½ cup chicken broth
3 tbsps white port
1 cup mushrooms, preferably
   Japanese enoki
   mushrooms
1 black truffle*

FOR THE SAUCE:
*2 shallots
1 cup red wine
1 cup Madeira
4 tsps balsamic or red wine
   vinegar*

TO SERVE:
*⅔ cup butter
2 tbsps whipping cream,
   whipped*

1. First make the creamy
vegetables. Peel the carrots
and kohlrabi. Trim and wash
the celery and leeks. Cut all
the vegetables into matchstick strips.
2. Melt the butter or margarine in a pot, and gently
fry the vegetables. Season
with salt and pepper, and
then stir in the cream, broth,
and port. Wipe the mush-
rooms. Cut the truffle into
thin strips. Add the mush-

Cut all the vegetables into
matchstick strips and fry gently in
the butter or margarine.

rooms, and truffle to the
cream mixture, and allow to
reduce slightly.
3. To make the red wine
sauce, peel and chop the
shallots. Mix together the
wine, Madeira, and vinegar
in a small pan. Bring to the
boil and allow to reduce to a
quarter.
4. Meanwhile, pat the beef
dry, and season. Heat the oil,
and brown both sides of the
beef. Lower the heat, and fry
for a further 5 minutes.
Remove the pan from the
heat and set aside.
5. Rub the reduced red wine
sauce through a sieve. Dice
½ cup of the butter, and beat
into the sauce, a few pieces
at a time. Mix the remaining
butter with the vegetables.
Finally fold the whipped
cream into the vegetables.
6. Serve the vegetables on a
warm dish and top with the
filets. Pour the sauce over
them.
Recommended   drink: a
fruity red wine.

TIP

*Enoki
mushrooms are a
Japanese
delicacy. They are
very tiny. If you
cannot find
them, use the
smallest button
mushrooms.*

BEEF FILET AND CHANTERELLES WRAPPED IN SWISS CHARD LEAVES

SERVES 4 ■ ■

Preparation and cooking time: 1 hour
Kcal per serving: 345
P = 21g, F = 26g, C = 8g

2 cups chanterelle
   mushrooms
2 shallots
3 tbsps butter
salt
freshly ground white pepper
⅓ cup heavy cream
3 tbsps minced parsley
1–2 tbsps breadcrumbs
4 beef filets (about 4 ounces
   each)
2 tbsps oil
4 large Swiss-chard leaves

Add sufficient breadcrumbs to the mushroom filling to bind the mixture together.

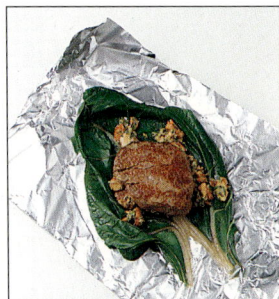
Wrap the beef filet first in a Swiss chard leaf and then a sheet of aluminum foil.

1. Wipe the chanterelles and cut into small pieces. Peel and chop the shallots. Melt the butter in a pot, and gently fry the chanterelles and shallots for 5 minutes. Season with salt and pepper, and stir in the cream. Bring to the boil and allow to reduce slightly. Stir in the parsley, and add sufficient breadcrumbs to bind the mixture, which should be of a workable consistency. Remove from the heat and set aside to cool.

> **TIP**
>
> *If chanterelles are not available, almost any wild or cultivated mushroom, such as shiitake or cloud ears, would be suitable for the filling.*

2. Pat the fillets dry, and season with salt and pepper. Heat the oil in a skillet, and fry the filet slices over a high heat for 2 minutes on each side. Remove and set aside to cool.
3. Bring a large pan of lightly salted water to the boil. Blanch the Swiss chard leaves, remove, and plunge them straight into ice-cold water. Lay the leaves out on a tea-towel and dry them well. Coat each leaf with some of the mushroom filling and place a filet slice on top. Wrap the filet tightly first in the Swiss chard leaf and then in a sheet of aluminum foil. Poach for 8–10 minutes in lightly boiling water.
Serving suggestions: chive sauce and small white turnips.
Recommended drink: a hearty white wine.

BEEF FILETS IN MORELLO CHERRY SAUCE

SERVES 4 ■ ■

Preparation and cooking time: 40 minutes
Kcal per serving: 450
P = 20g, F = 28g, C = 21g

1 cup baby onions
salt
freshly ground white pepper
1½ cups morello cherries
2 shallots
1 cup beef broth
½ cup red wine
½ cup kirsch or cherry
   brandy
4 tbsps port
4 slices beef filet (about 4
   ounces each)
4 tbsps grapeseed oil
1 tsp arrowroot
3 tbsps butter

Fry the filets in the oil, turning to brown both sides.

Add the remaining cherries to the sauce just before serving.

1. Peel the baby onions. Blanch in lightly salted boiling water for 1 minute. Drain. Wash and pit the cherries.
2. Peel and chop the shallots. Place the shallots, broth, wine, kirsch, or cherry brandy and port in a small pan, and bring to the boil over a high heat. Allow to reduce by a third.

> **TIP**
>
> *For best results, use fresh cherries for this dish, but in winter frozen or canned and drained morello cherries are a suitable alternative. This sauce also goes well with game.*

3. Meanwhile, pat the beef dry, and season with salt and pepper. Heat half the oil in a skillet, and fry the beef for about 2 minutes on each side. Remove from the pan, wrap in aluminum foil, and set aside to rest.
4. Add the remaining oil to the pan, and fry the baby onions over a high heat. Season with salt and pepper. Add 2 cups of the cherries and warm through.
5. Rub the reduced sauce through a sieve into a pan. Bring back to the boil and stir in the arrowroot. Dice the butter, and stir into the sauce, a few pieces at a time. Add the remaining cherries.
6. Place the steaks on warm plates and surround with the onions and cherries. Pour the sauce over them.
Serving suggestion: potato gnocchi with chopped hazelnuts.
Recommended drink: a medium red wine.

SLICED BEEF WITH SWEETCORN, BABY ONIONS, AND LONG-GRAIN RICE

SERVES 4 ■ ■ ■
Preparation and cooking time:
1 hour 20 minutes
Kcal per serving: 665
P = 32g, F = 33g, C = 55g

3 fresh corn-on-the-cob
salt
freshly ground white pepper
2 tbsps butter or margarine
1 cup long-grain rice
1 tbsp chopped shallots
4-5 cups beef broth
1 cup baby onions
1 pound beef filet
2 tbsps grapeseed oil
1 cup heavy cream
3 tbsps dry sherry
4 tsps sherry vinegar
2 tbsps whipped cream

1. Cook the corn cobs in plenty of salted water for 30–40 minutes or until tender. Scrape off all the kernels with a knife.
2. Melt the butter or margarine in a pan, and gently fry the rice and chopped shallots, for 5 minutes stirring constantly. Add a little broth, cover, and boil gently for 20 minutes, gradually adding more broth as the rice cooks. Depending on the quality of the rice, it will require 2-3 cups broth.
3. Peel the baby onions, and blanch for 1 minute in lightly salted water. Drain.
4. Pat the beef dry, and cut into thin strips. Season with salt and pepper. Heat the oil in a large pan and fry the beef strips, stirring frequently. Remove from the pan and keep warm. Add the sweetcorn kernels and baby onions to the pan, and gently fry. Season with salt and pepper. Remove from the pan and keep warm.

Fry the strips of beef until browned.

Fry the sweetcorn kernels and baby onions in the meat juices.

5. Add the remaining beef broth, cream, sherry and vinegar to the pan. Bring to the boil, and allow to reduce until the sauce becomes creamy. Return the meat and vegetables to the pan, bring to the boil, and then fold in the whipped cream.
6. Serve the sliced beef with the rice.
Serving suggestion: fresh green salad.
Recommended drink: a medium rosé wine.

BOILED BEEF IN HORSERADISH AND CAPER SAUCE

SERVES 4 ■
Preparation and cooking time: 15 minutes (not including meat cooking time)
Kcal per serving: 600
P = 20g, F = 56g, C = 3g

1½ pounds boiled beef
2 cups beef broth

FOR THE SAUCE:
2 egg yolks
4 tsps sherry vinegar
1 tsp French mustard
4 tbsps creamed horseradish
½ cup grapeseed oil
salt
freshly ground black pepper
1 cup sour cream
⅔ cup capers

1. Cut the meat into thin slices. Place in a pan with the broth, and warm through.
2. To make the sauce, beat together the egg yolks, vinegar, mustard, horseradish, and oil with a hand mixer to make a creamy mayonnaise. Season with salt and pepper, and stir in the sour cream, and capers.
3. Serve the sauce with the meat.
Serving suggestions: new potatoes and a green salad.
Recommended drink: a dry white wine.

TOP ROUND WITH A MUSHROOM CRUST

SERVES 4 ■ ■
Preparation and cooking time: 40 minutes
Kcal per serving: 445
P = 46g, F = 27g, C = 4g

1 x top round roast (about 1½ pounds)
salt
freshly ground white pepper
3 tbsps grapeseed oil
2 cups wild mushrooms, such as shiitake or oyster mushrooms
2 shallots
7 ounces beef marrow
2 egg yolks
3 tbsps minced parsley
1–2 tbsps breadcrumbs
1 tbsp Dijon mustard

1. Pat the meat dry, and season with salt and pepper. Heat the oil in a pot and brown the beef all over. Transfer the casserole to a preheated oven and cook at 400°F for 15 minutes, turning once.
2. Wipe and chop the mushrooms. Peel and chop the shallots. Cut the marrow into pieces. Place in a pan and heat through. Rub through a sieve into a skillet. Set over a low heat.
3. Gently cook the shallots, and mushrooms in the marrow, and season with salt and pepper. Remove the pan from the heat and set aside to cool. Stir the egg yolks, and parsley into the mushroom mixture. Add sufficient breadcrumbs to bind and create a workable mixture.
4. Coat the beef with mustard and then with the mushroom mixture. Brown the crust under a preheated broiler.
Serving suggestions: dauphinois potatoes and shallots with mustard.
Recommended drink: a full-

VEAL ROLLS

SERVES 4 ■ ■ ■
Preparation and cooking time: 1 hour 10 minutes
Kcal per serving: 745
P = 37g, F = 46g, C = 45g

4 veal filet slices (about 6 ounces each)
salt
freshly ground white pepper
bunch of fresh coriander (cilantro)
1 small, ripe mango
4 tbsps butter or margarine
4 tbsps ground cashew nuts
1-inch piece root ginger, peeled and grated
1 tsp ground turmeric
½ cup heavy cream
2 eggs, beaten
1 cup unsweetened shredded coconut

1. Pat the veal dry, and cut the fillets open lengthwise. Place between two sheets of parchment paper and pound with a meat hammer. Season with salt and pepper, and sprinkle with a few coriander leaves. Finely chop the remaining leaves.

TIP

Fresh coriander, or cilantro as it is often called, has a strong flavor, so it should be used sparingly. In South America and Asia, it is used in much the same way as Europeans use parsley.

2. Peel the mango, cut the flesh from the stone, and dice it. Melt 1 tbsp of the butter or margarine in a pot, and gently fry the mango for 2–3 minutes. Add the nuts and ginger, and season with salt, pepper, and turmeric.

Cover the veal filets first with coriander leaves, then with the mango mixture and finally roll them up tightly.

Stir in the cream and bring to the boil. Continue to boil until the liquid has evaporated. Stir in the chopped coriander, remove from the heat and set aside to cool.
3. Spread the mango mixture on the scallops and roll them up from the short end. Secure with cocktail sticks or trussing thread.
4. Whisk the eggs well. Dip the veal rolls first in the egg and then in the coconut. Press the coconut coating firmly to the rolls.
5. Melt the remaining butter in a ovenproof pot, and fry the veal rolls over a medium heat until they are browned all over. Transfer the pot to a preheated oven and cook at 400°F for 10 minutes.
Serving suggestions: Chinese (Nappa) cabbage in a light sherry sauce with a few pieces of mango and toasted coconut flakes.
Recommended drink: a medium red or white wine.

VEAL SCALLOPS WITH MOZZARELLA CHEESE AND TRUFFLE

SERVES 4 ■ ■
Preparation and cooking time: 30 minutes
Kcal per serving: 445
P = 39g, F = 19g, C = 29g

4 veal scallops (about 6 ounces each)
salt
freshly ground white pepper
1 cup Mozzarella cheese
1 black truffle or 2 tbsps truffle trimmings
2 eggs, beaten
1 cup breadcrumbs
4 tbsps butter

1. Ask your butcher to cut a "pocket" in the side of the scallops, or cut them open and carefully flatten them with the steak hammer. Season with salt and pepper.
2. Cut the Mozzarella cheese, and truffle into very thin slices. Stuff these slices into the "pockets." Alternatively, sandwich them between the halves of the scallop and secure the edges.
3. Dip the stuffed scallops first in the egg, and then in the breadcrumbs. Press the coating on firmly.
4. Melt the butter in a ovenproof pot, and fry the scallops on both sides over a medium heat until golden-brown. Transfer the casserole to a preheated oven and cook at 400°F for 10 minutes.
Serving suggestions: leaf spinach and a light cheese sauce.
Recommended drink: a full-bodied white wine.

SLICES OF VEAL WITH BEANS AND COCONUT

SERVES 4 ■ ■
Preparation and cooking time: 45 minutes
Kcal per serving: 550
P = 26g, F = 39g, C = 24g

14 ounces veal filet
1¼ cups broad beans
salt
freshly ground white pepper
3 tbsps grapeseed oil
½ cup fresh coconut flakes
milk from 1 coconut
1 cup beef broth
1 cup sour cream or crème fraîche
1 stalk lemongrass (or a little freshly grated root ginger)
2 tbsps torn basil leaves

1. Pat the veal dry, and cut into thin strips. Shell the broad beans, and blanch in boiling salted water for 1 minute. Drain, plunge the beans into cold water, and remove the outer green skin.
2. Season the veal with salt and pepper. Heat the oil in a skillet, and stir-fry the veal for 5 minutes. Remove from the pan, and set aside. Add the beans, and coconut flakes to the pan, and fry for 3–4 minutes. Season with salt and pepper. Return the veal to the pan. Add the coconut milk, broth and sour cream or crème fraîche. Bring to the boil, and allow to reduce until creamy.
3. Cut the lemongrass, if using, into thin strips. Stir the lemongrass or ginger, and basil into the veal mixture and serve immediately.
Serving suggestion: pasta.
Recommended drink: a medium dry white wine.

LAMB CURRY WITH EGGPLANT, ZUCCHINI AND TOMATOES

SERVES 4 ■ ■

Preparation and cooking time: 40 minutes
Kcal per serving: 440
P = 24g, F = 29g, C = 15g

2 large eggplants
4 large zucchini
1 onion
1 pound lean boneless lamb, diced
salt
freshly ground white pepper
1¾ cups canned tomatoes
1 garlic clove
1 red chili
4 tbsps olive oil
1-inch root ginger, peeled and grated
2 tsps curry powder
1 cup beef broth
½ cup dry white wine
4 tsps garlic or white wine vinegar

Season the lamb well, and then fry in olive oil.

Add the canned tomatoes last, and season again, if necessary.

1. Wash, trim, and dice the eggplant and zucchini. Peel and chop the onion. Season the lamb with salt and pepper.
2. Drain the tomatoes and reserve the juice. Peel and finely chop the garlic. Halve, seed, wash, and finely chop the chili.

3. Heat the oil in a large flameproof casserole, and fry the lamb, stirring frequently, until browned all over. Add the onions, eggplant and zucchini, and fry, stirring frequently, for 5 minutes. Season with salt and pepper, and stir in the ginger, curry powder, garlic and chili. Add the reserved tomato juice, broth, wine and vinegar. Cover and simmer for about 10 minutes. Add the tomatoes and adjust the seasoning, if necessary. Heat through and serve.
Serving suggestion: brown or long-grain rice or small, fried potatoes.
Recommended drink: a medium dry white wine.

> **TIP**
>
> *The bitter flavor of eggplant can be alleviated if they are sliced, sprinkled with salt, and left to drain for 30 minutes. Rinse, pat dry, and use according to the recipe.*

LOIN OF LAMB WITH PISTOU AU GRATIN

(photograph page 68)

SERVES 4 ■ ■

Preparation and cooking time: 30 minutes
Kcal per serving: 790
P = 19g, F = 79g, C = 0g

1 boned loin of lamb (about 1½ pounds)
salt
freshly ground white pepper
3 tbsps olive oil
2 tbsps Dijon mustard

FOR THE PISTOU:
2 garlic cloves
3 tbsps minced parsley
3 tbsps minced basil
3 tbsps minced chervil
1 tbsp rosemary leaves
1 tbsp thyme leaves
1 cup olive oil
salt
freshly ground white pepper
4–5 tbsps breadcrumbs

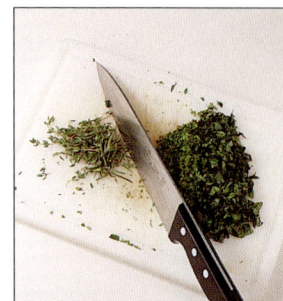
To make the pistou, finely chop the herbs and garlic cloves.

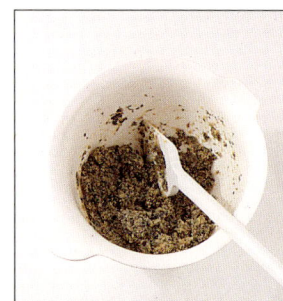
Add the oil, breadcrumbs and seasoning to make a creamy mixture.

1. Wash the lamb, and pat dry. Rub salt and pepper into the flesh. Heat the oil in a flameproof casserole, and brown the meat all over. Transfer the casserole to a preheated oven and cook at 400°F for 5 minutes.
2. Peel and mince the garlic. Mix together the parsley, basil, chervil, rosemary, thyme, garlic, and oil.

Coat the lamb first with mustard.

Season, and gradually add sufficient breadcrumbs to bind the mixture into a workable paste. Remove meat from oven.
3. Coat the lamb surface first with the mustard, and then with the pistou. Brown under a preheated broiler for a few minutes. Carve at table.
Serving suggestion: potato and zucchini fritters.
Recommended drink: a fruity red wine.

> **TIP**
>
> *The loin of lamb may be browned on the bone. It can then be boned, and the meat can be re-arranged on the backbone before being broiled with the pistou coating.*

Quick-and-easy Recipes

Meat just has to be the ideal ingredient if time is short. When you are in a hurry, you'll be looking for cuts which need only a short cooking time. Liver and chops spring to mind, but shoulder of pork and ribs can also be turned into delicious dishes both quickly and easily. Don't forget ground meat in the race against the clock; scallops and steaks are also strong candidates in this contest. The lover of fine, fast food may, of course, be put off by the higher prices of these cuts, but there are many tasty and economical options to choose from as well, and you can still finish with time to spare!

*Calf's Liver in Port Cream
(recipe page 84)*

BEEF SIRLOIN WITH A PARSLEY CRUST

SERVES 4   ■■

Preparation and cooking time: 30 minutes
Kcal per serving: 470
P = 40g, F = 31g, C = 8g

2 large marrow bones
3 tbsps vegetable oil
1¾ pounds beef sirloin
salt
freshly ground black pepper
4–6 tbsps minced flat-leaved
    parsley
6 tbsps breadcrumbs
pinch grated nutmeg
pinch cayenne pepper
1 tsp English mustard

1. Place the marrow bones in a bowl and cover with cold water, (this makes the marrow come out more easily.)
2. Heat the oil in a large pan, and fry the beef for about 10 minutes until browned all over. Season, and remove from the pan.
3. To make the herb paste, place the parsley in a bowl with the breadcrumbs. Squeeze the marrow from the bones into the bowl and mash with a fork. Season with salt, pepper, nutmeg, and cayenne. Stir in the mustard, and mix thoroughly.
4. Place the beef in an ovenproof dish, and coat the surface with the herb paste. Cook in a preheated oven at 475°F for 5–8 minutes, or until the crust is golden-brown. Double the cooking time, but lower the oven temperature to 375°F, if you prefer medium rather than rare beef.
5. To serve the meat, cut diagonally into finger-thick slices.
Serving suggestions: snowpeas and dauphinois potatoes.
Recommended drink: a robust red wine.

To remove the marrow more easily, soak the bones in cold water.

Fry the sirloin all over until well browned.

Mash the marrow with a fork, and mix well with the parsley, breadcrumbs, and spices.

Spread the herb paste over the beef and decorate with a pattern of diagonal lines made with the prongs of a fork.

BEEF FILET STEAKS WITH CAPER SAUCE

SERVES 4   ■

Preparation and cooking time: 15 minutes
Kcal per serving: 535
P = 38g, F = 40g, C = 2g

3 tbsps vegetable oil
4 beef filet steaks (about 6
    ounces each)
1 cup dry white wine
4 tbsps capers
1 cup heavy cream
salt
freshly ground white pepper
pinch cayenne pepper

1. Heat the oil, and fry the steaks over a high heat for 3 minutes on each side. Transfer to a platter, cover, and keep warm.
2. Pour off the oil. Add the wine to the pan, bring to the boil, and allow to reduce by a third.
3. Mix together the capers and cream and stir into the pan. Simmer for a further 3 minutes or until creamy. Season with salt, pepper and cayenne pepper.
4. Return the steaks, and meat juices to the pan and warm through over a low heat for about 5 minutes.
Serving suggestions: pasta shapes or rice and a tomato salad with basil.
Recommended drink: a light white wine.

ROUND STEAKS WITH A MUSTARD CRUST

SERVES 4   ■■

Preparation and cooking time: 25 minutes
Kcal per serving: 520
P = 38g, F = 40g, C = 2g

3 tbsps sunflower seeds
2 tbsps mustard
2 egg yolks
salt
freshly ground black pepper
½ tsp sweet paprika
4 round steaks (about 6
    ounces each)
3 tbsps vegetable oil

1. Crush the sunflower seeds finely in a grinder or with a pestle in a mortar.
2. Beat together the mustard and egg yolks, and stir in the ground sunflower seeds. Season with salt, pepper, and paprika.
3. Trim the steaks, and pat dry. Heat the oil, and fry the steaks over a high heat for 2–3 minutes on each side.
4. Remove the steaks from the pan, and place them on a baking sheet lined with aluminum foil. Spread the mustard paste evenly on top. Bake in a preheated oven at 475°F or cook under a preheated broiler for 3–5 minutes until golden-brown.
Serving suggestions: potato pancakes and tomato salad with green onions, and broccoli in cream.
Recommended drink: beer.

> **TIP**
>
> *For a spicier crust use Dijon mustard.*

STUFFED ROLLS OF VEAL WITH BASIL

SERVES 4 ■■
*Preparation and cooking
time: 35 minutes
Kcal per serving: 400
P = 42g, F = 19g, C = 6g*

3 bunches basil
2 tbsps breadcrumbs
2 egg yolks
salt
freshly ground black pepper
3 tbsps olive oil
4 thin veal scallops (about 6
    ounces each)
2 onions
1 cup dry white wine
3 tbsps sour cream
dash lemon juice
dash Worcestershire sauce

1. Rinse the basil and shake dry. Pick off the leaves, and reserve a few of the best for the garnish. Finely chop the remaining leaves.
2. Mix together the breadcrumbs and egg yolks, and season with salt and pepper. Add 1 tbsp of the olive oil, and stir well to make a smooth mixture.
3. Pound the veal scallops with a steak hammer. Pat dry and season both sides with salt and pepper. Spread the breadcrumb mixture on the scallops, roll up tightly, and secure with cocktail sticks or trussing thread.
4. Peel and finely chop the onions. Heat the remaining oil in a large skillet, and gently fry the veal rolls until browned all over. Add the onions, and fry until transparent. Pour in the white wine, cover, and cook for 20 minutes.
5. Remove the rolls from the pan. Beat the sour cream into the cooking liquid, bring to the boil, and season with salt and pepper. Add the lemon juice and Worcestershire sauce.

Rinse the basil, shake dry and chop finely.

Season the veal scallops, coat with the herb mixture, roll up, and secure with cocktail sticks.

Beat the sour cream into the cooking liquid, season, and add the lemon juice, and Worcestershire sauce.

6. Serve the veal rolls with the sauce on warmed plates, and garnish with the reserved basil leaves.
Other herbs may be used for the filling, and ground almonds are an alternative to breadcrumbs.
Serving suggestions: potato pancakes and a salad with cherry tomatoes.
Recommended drink: a hearty Italian red wine.

CALF'S LIVER IN PORT WINE CREAM SAUCE

(photograph page 80)

SERVES 4 ■
*Preparation and cooking
time: 25 minutes
Kcal per serving: 695
P = 37g, F = 44g, C = 23g*

1¾ pounds calf's liver
3 shallots
2 tbsps flour
3 tbsps butter
1 cup port
1 cup heavy cream
salt
freshly ground white pepper
½ tsp dried marjoram
2 tsps lemon juice
bunch of chervil

1. Place the calf's liver in tepid water for 2–3 minutes. Then pull off the skin, and cut into finger-thick slices. Peel and finely chop the shallots.
2. Sift the flour onto a plate and coat the liver slices.
3. Melt the butter in a large skillet, and fry the strips of liver, in batches if necessary, until browned all over. Remove, cover, and set aside.
4. Gently fry the shallots in the same pan until transparent. Add the port, bring to the boil, and allow to reduce by half.
5. Stir in the cream, and simmer gently for about 8 minutes until the sauce is creamy. Season with salt and pepper, and stir in the marjoram, and lemon juice.
6. Return the strips of liver to the pan and warm through for 2–3 minutes.
7. Meanwhile, rinse and dry the chervil. Remove the stalks and stir the leaves into the sauce before serving.
Serving suggestion: mashed potato.
Recommended drink: a light, dry white wine.

VEAL SCALLOPS WITH GRAPEFRUIT

SERVES 4 ■■
*Preparation and cooking
time: 30 minutes
Kcal per serving: 320
P = 37g, F = 12g, C = 15g*

4 scallops (6 ounces each)
2 tbsps butter
1 tbsp oil
salt
freshly ground white pepper
½ tsp grated nutmeg
2 pink grapefruit
4 tsps Cointreau
1 tbsp chopped pistachio nuts

1. Make a deep cut in the side of the veal scallops, open them out, and flatten with a steak hammer. Pat dry.
2. Heat the butter and oil in a large skillet, and fry the scallops over a high heat for 1 minute on each side. Season with salt, pepper, and a little nutmeg. Remove from the pan, cover, and set aside.
3. Squeeze the juice from one grapefruit, and mix together with the Cointreau. Pour into the pan, and allow to reduce by a third over a gentle heat.
4. Meanwhile, peel the second grapefruit and remove the white parts, and inner skin. With a sharp knife, cut the flesh into segments.
5. Season the sauce with salt, pepper, and a little nutmeg. Return the meat, and meat juices to the pan, and warm through.
6. Arrange the grapefruit segments on 4 plates, place the veal scallops beside them, and sprinkle with the pistachio nuts.
Serving suggestions: rice and salad.
Recommended drink: a light, dry white wine.

PORK FILET WITH HERB SAUCE

SERVES 4 ■
Preparation and cooking time: 30 minutes
Kcal per serving: 500
P = 42g, F = 36g, C = 2g

1¾ pounds pork filet
3 tbsps oil
salt
freshly ground black pepper
pinch freshly grated nutmeg
¾ cup meat broth
7 ounces cream cheese with herbs
2 garlic cloves
dash lemon juice
3 tbsps finely chopped fresh mixed herbs

1. Trim the pork, rinse, and pat dry. Heat the oil in a large skillet, and fry the pork until browned all over. Season with salt, pepper and a little nutmeg. Cover, and cook for 15 minutes.
2. Remove the pork from the pan, cover, and set aside. Pour off the fat. Add the broth to the pan over a low heat, scraping the pan to deglaze it.
3. Add the cream cheese, stirring constantly until it has melted. Peel and crush the garlic and add to the sauce. Simmer for about 3 minutes. Season with salt, pepper and lemon juice. Stir in the herbs.
4. Return the pork, and the meat juices to the pan, and simmer again for a further 3 minutes.
5. Cut the filet into ¼-inch slices, and arrange in a fan-shaped pattern on 4 plates. Pour the herb sauce over it.
Serving suggestion: baked potatoes.
Recommended drink: a light white wine.

Finely chopped fresh herbs give the sauce extra flavor.

Brown the beef filet all over in hot oil.

Add the cream cheese to the sauce allowing plenty of time for it to melt.

Finally, stir the herbs and spices into the cheese sauce.

CURRIED PORK WITH TOMATOES

SERVES 4 ■
Preparation and cooking time: 30 minutes
Kcal per serving: 655
P = 34g, F = 54g, C = 8g

1¾ pounds boneless pork shoulder
1 large onion
3 tbsps oil
2 tbsps curry powder
salt
freshly ground black pepper
3½ cups canned tomatoes
1 bayleaf
½ bunch green onions (scallions)

1. Cut the pork into ½-inch cubes. Peel and mince the onion. Heat the oil in a large skillet, and fry the pork over a high heat until browned all over.
2. Add the onion and curry powder, and gently fry for a further 5 minutes. Season with salt and pepper.
3. Add the tomatoes, can juice, and bayleaf. Bring to the boil, cover, and simmer for 20 minutes.
4. Meanwhile, wash and trim the green onions. Slice into thin rings.
5. Taste the curry and, if necessary, add a little more seasoning.
Serving suggestion: buttered rice with flaked almonds, and a green salad with a herb vinaigrette.
Recommended drink: a dry rosé wine.

PORK SCALOPPINI WITH TUNAFISH SAUCE

SERVES 4 ■ ■
Preparation and cooking time: 30 minutes
Kcal per serving: 655
P = 50g, F = 47g, C = 3g

3 tbsps butter
4 pork scallops
salt
freshly ground white pepper
½ cup dry white wine
7 ounce can of tuna fish
1 cup heavy cream
3 anchovy fillets, soaked
2 tsps wine vinegar
juice of ½ lime
2 tbsps finely chopped chervil

1. Melt the butter in a skillet, and fry the meat for 3 minutes

Purée the sauce with a hand-held mixer.

on each side. Remove from the pan, season, set aside and keep warm.
2. Pour off the fat. Add the wine to the pan over a low heat, scraping the pan to deglaze it.
3. Drain the tuna. Add to the pan, and break it up with a fork. Stir in the cream, and bring to the boil. Finely chop the anchovy fillets and add.
4. Purée the sauce with a hand-held mixer, and heat through. Season, and stir in the vinegar, and lime juice.
5. Place the scallops on 4 plates, pour the sauce over them and sprinkle with chervil.
Serving suggestion: French bread.

PORK SCALOPPINI WITH MOZZARELLA

SERVES 4 ■

Preparation and cooking time: 20 minutes
Kcal per serving: 480
P = 47g, F = 32g, C = 1g

2 tbsps butter
2 tbsps olive oil
4 pork scallops (about 6 ounces each)
salt
freshly ground black pepper
4 garlic cloves
½ bunch basil
⅔ cup Mozzarella cheese

1. Heat the butter and olive oil in a large skillet. Pat the pork dry, and fry for 2 minutes on each side. Season with salt and pepper.
2. Arrange the scallops side by side in an ovenproof dish or on a baking sheet.
3. Peel and crush the garlic. Spread the crushed garlic on the pork. Rinse the basil, and shake dry. Pick the leaves from the stalks, and sprinkle over the meat, reserving a few leaves for the garnish. Cut the Mozzarella cheese into 8 slices. Top each scallop with 2 slices of cheese. Season with salt and pepper, and drizzle with the olive oil.
4. Bake in a preheated oven at 475°F until the cheese begins to melt. Remove from the oven, and transfer to a serving platter. Garnish with the reserved basil leaves.
Serving suggestions: rocket and cherry tomato salad with warm white bread.
Recommended drink: a fresh, light white wine.

Heat the butter and olive oil.

Season the scallops with salt and pepper and spread with crushed garlic.

Cut the Mozzarella cheese into 8 slices.

Cover the pork scallops first with basil and then Mozzarella.

HOT SPICED PORK WITH SWEETCORN

SERVES 4 ■

Preparation and cooking time: 35 minutes
Kcal per serving: 395
P = 28g, F = 21g, C = 22g

1½ pounds pork loin
3 tbsps oil
3 garlic cloves
1 large onion
2 green or red chilies
2½ cups canned tomatoes, chopped
1 cup canned sweetcorn
thyme sprig
salt
freshly ground black pepper

1. Rinse the pork, and pat dry. Cut into ¾-inch cubes. Heat the oil, and fry the pork, in batches, until brown.
2. Peel and crush the garlic. Peel, and chop the onion. Add the garlic and onion to the pan, and fry for a further 5 minutes.
3. Halve, seed, and wash the chilies. Cut into thin rings, and add to the pan. Stir in the tomatoes with their can juice. Cover and cook for 10 minutes.
4. Drain the sweetcorn. Stir the sweetcorn, and thyme into the pan, cover, and cook for a further 10 minutes.
5. Season with salt and pepper. Remove and discard thyme before serving.
Serving suggestions: buttered rice with chopped green pistachios, and a mixed green salad with a yogurt dressing.
Recommended drink: beer or red wine.

PORK CHOPS IN RED WINE SAUCE

SERVES 4 ■

Preparation and cooking time: 20 minutes
Kcal per serving: 525
P = 31g, F = 35g, C = 5g

4 pork chops (about 6 ounces each), trimmed of excess fat
3 tbsps oil
salt
freshly ground black pepper
1 large onion
2 slices smoked, streaky bacon, rinded
2 tsps all-purpose flour
1¾ cups dry red wine
1 tsp dried marjoram

1. Pat the chops dry. Heat the oil in a pan, and fry the chops for 4 minutes on each side. Season with salt and pepper, remove from the pan, cover, and set aside.
2. Peel and finely chop the onion. Fry the onion in the same pan until transparent.
3. Dice the bacon. Add the bacon to the pan, and fry for 5 minutes over a medium heat.
4. Sprinkle with the flour, and cook, stirring constantly, for 2 minutes. Stir in the wine. Sprinkle with the marjoram, and simmer for a further 5 minutes. Season with salt and pepper. Return the chops, and their juices to the pan and warm through in the sauce.
5. Arrange the pork chops with the sauce on warm plates.
Serving suggestion: mashed potato.
Recommended drink: a dry red wine.

PORK SCALOPPINI IN PARMESAN CHEESE

SERVES 4 ■■
Preparation and cooking time: 25 minutes
Kcal per serving: 485
P = 46g, F = 31g, C = 6g

4 tbsps breadcrumbs
4 tbsps grated Parmesan
  cheese
1 egg
4 thin pork scallops (about 6
  ounces each)
salt
freshly ground black pepper
2 garlic cloves
3 tbsps sunflower oil
1 lemon

1. Mix together the breadcrumbs and Parmesan cheese in a shallow bowl. Beat the egg in another shallow bowl.
2. Flatten the pork scallops with a steak hammer, and pat dry. Cut each scallop in half.
3. Season the meat with salt and pepper, and then dip the slices first in the beaten egg, and then in the breadcrumb-and-cheese mixture. Press the coating firmly in place.
4. Peel and quarter the garlic cloves. Heat the oil in a pan, fry the garlic until brown. Remove from the pan and discard. Fry the scallops in the garlic oil over a medium heat for 3 minutes on each side.
5. Cut the lemon into 8. Transfer the scallops to a serving dish and garnish with the lemon.
Cheese-coated pork scallops can be eaten hot or cold.
Serving suggestion: potato-and-cucumber salad, or steamed Swiss chard with mashed potatoes.
Recommended drink: a dry rosé wine.

Coat the pork scallops in the breadcrumb and cheese mixture.

Quarter the garlic cloves and fry them in oil until golden-brown.

Fry the breaded scallops in the garlic oil for a total of 6 minutes.

PORK CHOPS STUFFED WITH FETA CHEESE

SERVES 4 ■■
Preparation and cooking time: 30 minutes
Kcal per serving: 440
P = 32g, F = 34g, C = 2g

4 slices feta cheese
4 tbsps pitted green olives
1 garlic clove
salt
freshly ground black pepper
4 pork chops (about 8 ounces
  each)
3 tbsps vegetable oil
1 lemon

1. Mash the feta cheese with a fork.
2. Coarsely chop the olives and mix with the cheese. Peel and crush the garlic, and combine with the cheese and olives. Season with salt and pepper.
3. Cut a slit in the side of the pork chops and stuff each "pocket" with the cheese mixture. Sew up the opening with trussing thread.
4. Heat the oil in a large skillet, and fry the chops for about 4 minutes on each side. Season with salt and pepper.
5. Quarter the lemon and serve the segments with the pork chops.
If preferred, chopped onion and a few mixed herbs may be added to the feta cheese mixture.
Serving suggestions: roast potatoes or sesame seed rolls and a cucumber salad with onion, dill and yogurt dressing.
Recommended drink: a dry white wine.

Mash the feta cheese with a fork.

Coarsely chop the olives with a sharp knife.

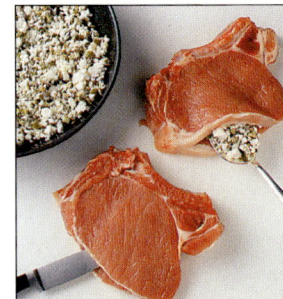

Spoon the seasoned cheese mixture into the "pockets."

Sew up the openings with trussing thread.

LAMB RAGOÛT WITH ALMONDS AND MINT

SERVES 4 ■

Preparation and cooking time: 30 minutes
Kcal per serving: 840
P = 39g, F = 73g, C = 7g

1¾ pounds leg or loin of lamb
1 large onion
3 tbsps butter
juice and peel of 1 lemon
⅔ cup ground almonds
1 cup heavy cream
1 cup lamb broth
salt
freshly ground white pepper
pinch ground cumin
1 tsp chopped root ginger
bunch of fresh mint

1. Rinse the lamb, and pat dry. Cut into slices and then into strips. Peel and finely chop the onion. Melt the butter in a large skillet, and fry the lamb strips, in batches if necessary, until browned all over. Remove from the pan, cover, and set aside.
2. Fry the onion in the same pan. Add the lemon juice, and peel, and bring to the boil. Stir in the almonds, and cook for a further 3 minutes. Add the cream and stock, and bring to the boil.
3. Return the meat to the pan. Season with salt, pepper, cumin, and ginger, and simmer for 15 minutes.
4. Meanwhile, rinse the mint, and shake dry. Tear off the leaves and mix with the lamb.
Serving suggestions: curried rice with raisins, and a green salad.
Recommended drink: a hearty red wine.

LAMB CUTLETS WITH CUCUMBER

SERVES 4 ■

Preparation and cooking time: 25 minutes
Kcal per serving: 745
P = 23g, F = 71g, C = 3g

2 cucumbers
2 tbsps butter
2 garlic cloves
salt
freshly ground white pepper
6 tbsps sour cream
3 tbsps minced dill
3 tbsps olive oil
8 lamb cutlets (about 4 ounces each)
2 tsps finely chopped rosemary

1. Peel the cucumbers, cut in half lengthwise and scrape out the seeds with a spoon. Cut the halves into very thin slices.
2. Melt the butter in a pan, and gently fry the cucumber for about 5 minutes. Peel and chop the garlic. Add the garlic to the pan, and stir well. Season with salt and pepper. Stir in the sour cream, and cook for a further 5 minutes. Stir in the dill.
3. Heat the oil in a large skillet, and fry the lamb cutlets for 2–3 minutes on each side. After turning the meat, season with salt and pepper and sprinkle with the rosemary.
4. Transfer the cutlets to a warm serving dish, arrange the cucumber around them, and serve.
Serving suggestion: small, roast potatoes or sesame seed rolls.
Recommended drink: strong red wine.

Peel the cucumber, cut in half lengthwise and slice thinly.

Season the cucumber with salt and pepper, add two crushed garlic cloves, and the sour cream, and cook for 5 minutes.

Add minced dill to the cucumber.

Brown the lamb cutlets in olive oil. Season with salt, pepper and rosemary.

LAMB AND RED PEPPERS

SERVES 4 ■

Preparation and cooking time: 25 minutes
Kcal per serving: 530
P = 28g, F = 44g, C = 4g

1¾ pounds boneless leg or loin of lamb
3 tbsps olive oil
1 large onion
3 garlic cloves
1 small can red pimientos
1 chili pepper
salt
freshly ground black pepper
pinch cayenne pepper
1 tsp sweet paprika
3 tbsps tomato paste
4 tbsps crème fraîche
juice of ½ lemon
3 tbsps minced flat-leaved parsley
parsley leaves to garnish (optional)

1. Rinse the lamb, and pat dry. Cut into slices and then into finger-thick strips.
2. Heat the olive oil in a large saucepan, and fry the meat, in batches if necessary, until browned all over.
3. Peel and finely chop the onion. Peel and crush the garlic. Add the onion, and garlic to the pan, and fry for a further 5 minutes.
4. Drain the pimientos and cut them into matchstick strips. Deseed and chop the chili. Stir the pimientos and chili into the pan, and season with salt, pepper, cayenne pepper and paprika. Stir in the tomato paste, crème fraîche, and lemon juice, lower the heat and simmer gently for 10 minutes.
5. Stir in the minced parsley. If liked, garnish with a few flat-leaved parsley leaves before serving.
Serving suggestion: croquette potatoes.

Microwave Recipes

*N*ew recipes have been developed that ensure that meat cooked in the microwave oven is not tough or dry. Those home cooks with combination ovens will certainly derive the greatest benefit from this quick way of cooking meat. Joints and filets can be cooked in a basic microwave, but the heat of a conventional oven or a broiler is necessary for a well-browned finish. Whichever method is chosen, remember that special microwave-safe cooking utensils are essential! Whatever the cut of meat, modern kitchen technology ensures that the cooked meat is tender and retains its natural flavor. Use salt sparingly, replacing it with the herbs and spices which will enhance the natural flavors. All recipes are for a standard 600 watt microwave, except where a combination microwave oven is specified.

Veal in Curry Sauce
(recipe page 99)

BOILED BEEF WITH SPRING VEGETABLES

SERVES 2
Standard microwave oven
Preparation and cooking
time: 45 minutes
Kcal per serving: 435
P = 46g, F = 21g, C = 15g

2 cups water
1 T-bone steak (about 1¼
    pounds)
salt
freshly ground black pepper
4 carrots, preferably with
    tops
4 green onions (scallions)
2 sticks celery
½ cup snowpeas
1 tbsp minced parsley

1. Pour the water into a microwave-safe dish large enough to take the meat and vegetables. Heat the water on *HIGH for 3–4 minutes.* Season the meat with salt and pepper. Place the steak in the hot water and cook on *HIGH for 15 minutes.*

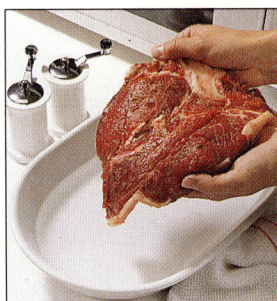

Place the seasoned beef in the hot water.

Arrange the vegetables around the beef and baste with the cooking liquid.

Miniature corn cobs could be added to the snowpeas.

TIP

The meat must have been well hung; the flesh should be deep red in color. If not, allow more time before adding the vegetables.

---

2. Meanwhile, peel the carrots, but leave a short length of the green tops. Trim the green onions, and remove the last third of the green leaves. Trim and wash the celery, and cut into matchstick strips. Trim the snowpeas.
3. Turn the meat over. Arrange the carrots, onions, and celery around the sides, season with salt and baste with a little of the cooking liquid. Cover and cook on *HIGH for 8–10 minutes.* Add the snowpeas, and cook on *HIGH for a further 5 minutes.*
4. Leave the meat to stand for a few minutes, sprinkle with parsley, and serve in the dish.
Serving suggestion: boiled potatoes.
Recommended drink: a medium white wine.

MEATBALLS IN PAPRIKA SAUCE

SERVES 4
Standard microwave oven
Preparation and cooking
time: 40 minutes
Kcal per serving: 370
P = 26g, F = 22g, C = 16g

1 onion
2 garlic cloves
3 tbsps vegetable oil
1 small red bell pepper
1 small yellow bell pepper
1 small green pepper
3 beefsteak tomatoes
salt
freshly ground black pepper
1 tbsp sweet paprika
1 thyme sprig
1 rosemary sprig
½ cup meat broth
1 bread roll or thick slice
    white bread
1 egg
1 tbsp chopped fresh parsley
12 ounces ground beef
1 tsp strong made mustard

1. Peel and chop the onion and garlic. Place the onion, garlic, and oil in a microwave-safe dish, and cook on *HIGH for 3–4 minutes* until transparent. Reserve 2 tbsps of the onion mixture.
2. Halve, seed, wash, and dice the peppers. Cut crosses in the tomato skins, dip in water, cover, and cook on *HIGH for 3–4 minutes.* Rinse and skin. Quarter, seed, and dice.
3. Stir the peppers and tomatoes into the onions, and season with salt, pepper, and paprika. Add the herbs and broth, cover and cook on *HIGH for 10–12 minutes.*
4. To prepare the meatballs, place the roll or bread in a bowl, cover with lukewarm water, and set aside to soak. Mix together the reserved onions, egg, parsley, and ground beef. Squeeze the water from the roll or bread, and add to the meatball mixture. Knead thoroughly to

The best time of year for peppers is from August to October.

Pour broth over the chopped, seasoned vegetables, cover, and cook.

make a smooth workable mixture. Season with salt, pepper, and add the mustard.
5. Shape the mixture into 12 meatballs, and place in the pepper sauce. Cover and cook on *HIGH for 3–5 minutes.* Leave to stand for a few minutes. If required, sprinkle with parsley.
Serving suggestions: penne, or other large pasta shapes, and a salad.
Recommended drink: a light Italian red wine.

CALF'S SWEETBREADS IN VEGETABLES

SERVES 2 ■ ■
*Standard microwave oven
Preparation and cooking
time: 35 minutes
Resting time: 2 hours
Kcal per serving: 415
P = 31g, F = 23g, C = 12g*

10 ounces calf's sweetbreads
2 green onions (scallions)
2 carrots
2 sticks celery
1 cup mushrooms
3 tbsps butter
½ cup veal broth
½ cup dry white wine
salt
freshly ground white pepper
1 tbsp chopped fresh herbs

1. Place the sweetbreads in a bowl and cover with cold water. Set aside to soak, changing the water frequently until the water remains clear and the sweetbreads are white. Drain and trim.
2. Trim and wash the green onions, and cut into matchstick strips. Peel the carrots and cut into matchstick strips. Trim and wash the celery and cut into matchstick strips. Wipe and slice the mushrooms.
3. Place the butter in a microwave-safe dish and melt on *HIGH for 2–3 minutes*. Stir the onions, carrots, celery, and mushrooms into the butter, cover and cook on *HIGH for 3–4 minutes*.
4. Add the wine and broth, and season with salt and pepper. Cover and cook on *HIGH for 4–5 minutes*.
5. Add sweetbreads, and spoon this over some vegetables. Cook on *MEDIUM for 5–6 minutes*. Leave to stand for a few minutes. Sprinkle with the herbs and serve.
Serving suggestion: boiled potatoes.
Recommended drink: a fruity red wine.

VEAL IN CURRY SAUCE

(photograph page 94)

SERVES 4 ■
*Standard microwave oven
Preparation and cooking
time: 30 minutes
Marinate for 1 hour
Kcal per serving: 320
P = 23g, F = 19g, C = 5g*

14 ounces lean boneless veal
½-inch piece root ginger
1 small piece of dried chili
2 tbsps soy sauce
4 tbsps rice wine or dry
    sherry
1 leek
1 cup mushrooms
3 tbsps oil
⅔ cup heavy cream
1 tbsp curry powder
salt
freshly ground white pepper
1 tsp cornstarch
4 tbsps chicken broth
coriander (cilantro) leaves
    (optional)

1. Rinse the veal and pat dry. Cut into thin strips and place in a bowl. Finely grate the ginger, and crush the chili. Mix together the ginger, chilli, soy sauce, and rice wine or sherry. Pour this over the veal strips and stir well. Cover and set aside to marinate for about an hour.
2. Meanwhile, trim and wash the leek, and cut into matchstick strips. Wipe and thinly slice the mushrooms.
3. Mix together the oil, leek, and mushrooms in a large microwave-safe dish and cook on *HIGH for 5–6 minutes*, stirring frequently.
4. Add the veal, marinade, and cream. Stir in the curry powder, and season with salt and pepper. Stir thoroughly. Cover and cook on *HIGH for 5–6 minutes*.
5. Stir the cornstarch into the chicken broth to make a smooth paste. Stir the paste into the veal and vegetable mixture. Cook on *HIGH for*

Mix together the grated ginger, chili, soy sauce, and sherry. Marinate the veal strips in the mixture.

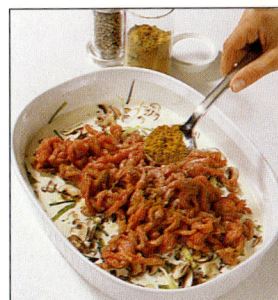

Sprinkle the veal with curry powder.

3–4 minutes. If liked, sprinkle with coriander leaves. Soy beansprouts or a few snowpeas can be included in the vegetable mixture.
Serving suggestion: fluffy rice.
Recommended drink: a fruity Italian white wine.

VEAL RAGOÛT WITH ANCHOVIES

SERVES 4 ■
*Standard microwave oven
Preparation and cooking
time: 40 minutes
Kcal per serving: 235
P = 24g, F = 12g, C = 7g*

14 ounces veal round
1 large onion
3 sticks celery
2 small zucchini
3 beefsteak tomatoes
3–4 chopped anchovies
1 small piece of dried chili
salt
freshly ground white pepper
1 tsp sweet paprika
4 tbsps olive oil
juice of 1 lemon

1. Rinse the veal and pat dry. Cut into ¾-inch cubes. Peel and chop the onion. Trim and chop the celery and zucchini. Blanch, skin, seed, and chop the beefsteak tomatoes.
2. Chop the anchovies. Mix together the chili, anchovies, veal, onion, celery, zucchini, and tomatoes in a large microwave-safe dish. Season with salt, pepper, and paprika. Add the oil and lemon juice, cover and cook on *HIGH for 18–20 minutes*. Stir well before serving.
Serving suggestion: noodles.
Recommended drink: a Spanish rosé.

> **TIP**
>
> *This ragoût is ideal for hot summer days, as it also tastes delicious cold.*

STUFFED BREAST OF PORK WITH PRUNES AND WALNUTS

SERVES 8 ■■

Combination microwave oven
Preparation and cooking time: 1 hour 40 minutes
Kcal per serving: 415
P = 45g, F = 14g, C = 19g

4½ pounds breast of pork
salt
freshly ground black pepper

FOR THE STUFFING:
3 day-old bread rolls
1 cup milk
½ cup prunes, pitted
½ cup brandy
2 egg yolks
salt
freshly ground black pepper
pinch ground cinnamon
grated rind of ½ orange
4 tbsps walnuts, chopped
1 tbsp minced parsley
1–2 tbsps breadcrumbs

TO SERVE:
1 cup meat broth
2 tbsps crème fraîche

1. Ask your butcher to cut a "pocket" in the breast of pork. Rinse the meat, pat dry, and rub salt and pepper into the flesh, including inside the "pocket."
2. To make the stuffing, cut the rolls into slices. Warm the milk on *HIGH for 1–2 minutes*, and pour it over the bread. Chop the prunes and place in a microwave-safe dish. Add the brandy and cook on *MEDIUM for 2–3 minutes*. Drain the prunes and reserve the brandy.
3. Squeeze milk from the bread. Work bread to a smooth paste in a blender with half the prunes. Add remaining prunes and egg yolks, and season with salt and pepper. Stir in the cinnamon, orange rind, walnuts, and parsley and, if the mixture is too soft, add a few breadcrumbs.

Squeeze the milk from the rolls and purée them with half the drained prunes.

4. Reserve a little stuffing and spoon the remainder into the breast of pork. Secure the opening with trussing thread and place in an ovenproof, microwave-safe dish. Place the reserved stuffing alongside and cook on *MEDIUM for 15 minutes* in a combination microwave preheated to 425°F (fan-assisted 400°F). Add the broth and reserved brandy and cook on *LOW for 40–45 minutes* at 400°F (fan-assisted 350°F).
5. Remove the pork, cover with aluminum foil, and leave to rest. Stir the crème fraîche into the sauce, reduce on *HIGH for 5 minutes*. Rub the sauce through a sieve.
6. Cut the pork into slices with a sharp knife. Serve the sauce separately.
Serving suggestions: dumplings and broccoli.
Recommended drink: a full-bodied red wine.

PORK FILET WITH GORGONZOLA SAUCE

SERVES 2 ■

Combination microwave oven
Preparation and cooking time: 20 minutes
Kcal per serving: 595
P = 39g, F = 45g, C = 2g

1 pork filet (about 10 ounces)
salt
freshly ground black pepper
2 shallots
1 tbsp vegetable oil
1 tbsp butter
4 tsps dry sherry
1 tsp sherry vinegar
½ cup Gorgonzola cheese
3 tbsps heavy cream
1 tbsp chopped fresh parsley

1. Rinse the pork and pat dry. Rub salt and pepper into the meat. Peel and chop the shallots.
2. Place the oil, butter, and shallots in a microwave-safe dish and cook *on HIGH for 3–4 minutes* until transparent. Coat the pork with the melted butter and shallots, and pour the sherry, and vinegar over it. Cover the dish and cook on *HIGH for 3–4 minutes*.
3. Purée the cream and cheese in a blender. Coat the pork with the Gorgonzola cream.
4. Switch on the broiler and cook on *HIGH for 4–5 minutes*. Leave to stand for a few minutes and then sprinkle with parsley.
If the sauce is too thin, reduce it by boiling for *a few minutes on HIGH*. In the meantime, keep the meat warm.
Serving suggestions: fettuccini, and young green beans.
Recommended drink: a dry white wine.

ROAST PORK WITH HERBS

SERVES 6–8 ■

Combination microwave oven
Preparation and cooking time: 1¼ hours
Kcal per serving if serving 6: 410
P = 38g, F = 26g, C = 1g

3½ pounds loin of pork with bones
2 thyme sprigs
1 oregano sprig
2 basil sprigs
3 sage leaves
2 tarragon leaves
bunch of parsley
2 garlic cloves
1 onion
2 tbsps herb mustard
salt
freshly ground black pepper
½ cup dry white wine

1. Ask your butcher to remove the meat from the backbone but keep the bones.
2. Chop the thyme, oregano, basil, sage, tarragon, and parsley. Peel and chop the garlic and onion. Mix together the chopped herbs, garlic, onion, and mustard.
3. Rinse the pork and pat dry. Rub salt and pepper into the flesh, and coat with the herb paste. Place the meat on its backbone. Cook on a roasting sheet with a drip pan underneath on *LOW for 50-55 minutes* in a combination microwave preheated to 400°F (fan-assisted 350°F) until crisp.
4. Remove the pork, cover, and leave to stand. Add the white wine to the meat juices and cook on *HIGH for 4-5 minutes*.
5. Cut the pork into slices and serve the wine and herb sauce separately.
Serving suggestion: baked potatoes with soured cream.
Recommended drink: cold beer.

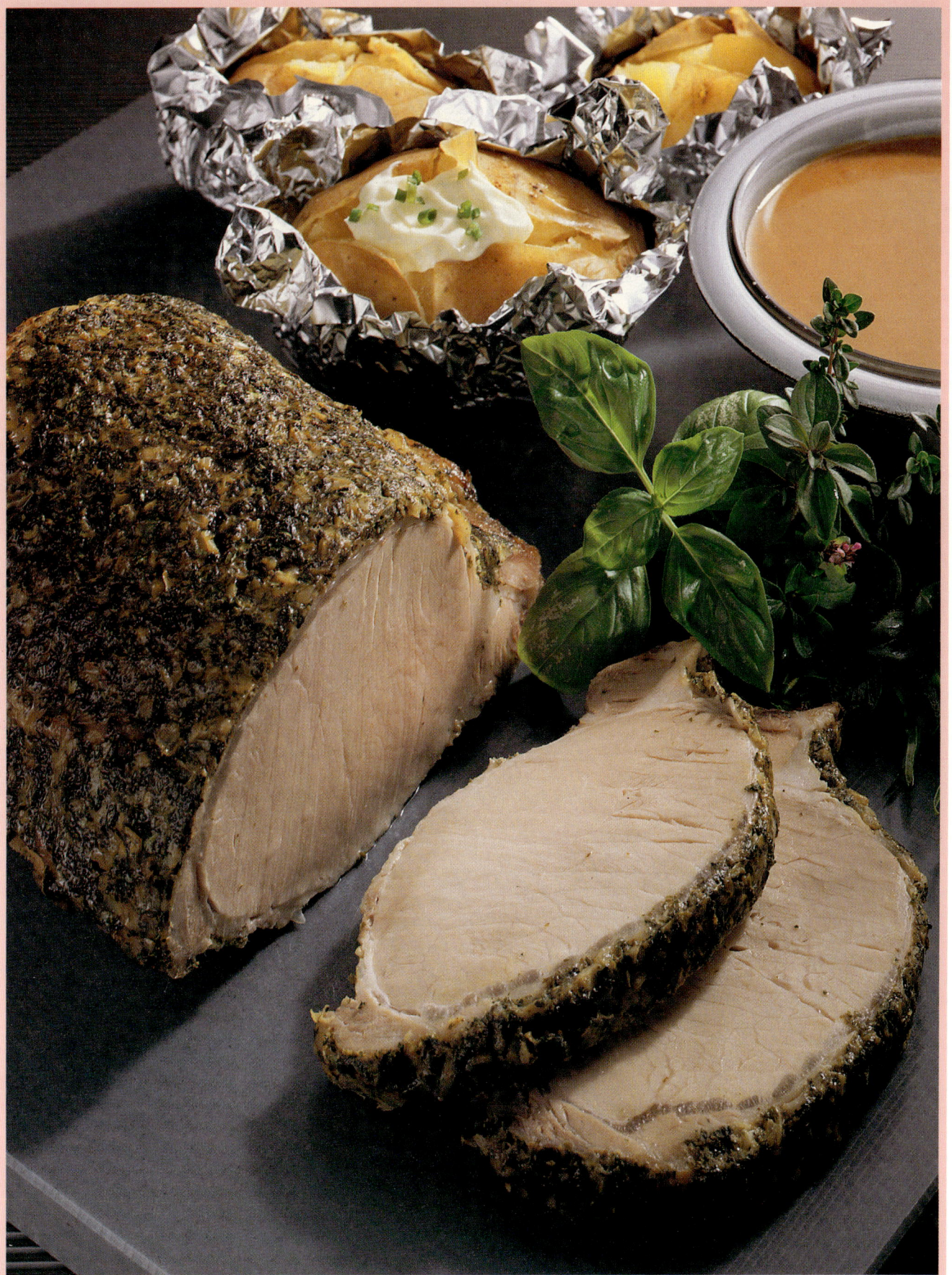

SHOULDER OF SUCKLING PIG WITH HONEY AND APRICOT SAUCE

SERVES 6 ■
Combination microwave oven
Preparation and cooking time: 1 hour 20 minutes
Kcal per serving: 740
P = 44g, F = 57g, C = 10g

4½ pounds suckling pig
salt
freshly ground black pepper
6–8 cloves
1 tbsp hot mustard
2 tbsps clear honey
grated rind of ½ orange
1 tsp grated root ginger
½ tsp ground cinnamon
pinch cayenne pepper
½ cup white wine
½ cup veal broth
1 cup apricots

Brush the top surface of the seasoned meat with the mustard and honey mixture.

Pour the wine and honey mixture over the pork shoulder and apricots.

1. Ask your butcher to score a diamond pattern in the pork rind. Wash the meat and pat dry. Rub the flesh with salt and pepper. Stud the pork with cloves, and place in a large, ovenproof microwave-safe dish.

2. Stir together the mustard, honey, orange rind, ginger, cinnamon, and cayenne pepper, and season with salt and pepper. Brush the mixture over the pork rind. Combine the remainder with the wine and broth.

3. Cook the shoulder, with the rind facing downwards, on *MEDIUM for 20 minutes* in a combination microwave preheated to 400°F (fan-assisted 350°F).

4. Meanwhile, wash, halve, and pit the apricots.

5. Turn the shoulder over, arrange the apricots around the roast, and pour over half the wine-and-honey mixture. Cook for a further *20 minutes on MEDIUM at 350°F (fan-assisted 325°F)*. Baste the shoulder with the remaining wine-and-honey mixture, and cook on the same setting for a further 10 minutes.

6. Remove the meat, cover with aluminum foil, and keep warm. Strain the sauce through a sieve. Cut the meat into slices and hand the sauce separately.

Serving suggestions: boiled potatoes and Brussels sprouts.

Recommended drink: a fruity white wine.

ROAST PORK WITH ORANGE AND RAISIN SAUCE

SERVES 4 ■
Combination microwave oven
Preparation and cooking time: 1 hour
Marinate for several hours
Kcal per serving: 555
P = 38g, F = 31g, C = 21g

1¾ pounds boneless neck of pork
salt
freshly ground white pepper
1 tsp chopped fresh rosemary
2 tbsps orange marmalade
grated rind of 1 orange
1 tbsp hot mustard
5 tbsps medium dry sherry
4 tbsps raisins
juice of 1–2 oranges

Brush the meat with the orange marinade and leave for a few hours.

After about 10 minutes, add the orange juice to the dish.

1. Rinse the pork and pat dry. Rub salt and pepper into the flesh. Mix together the rosemary, marmalade, orange rind, mustard, and half the sherry. Place the pork in an ovenproof, microwave-safe dish. Brush the surface with the marinade, cover with aluminum foil, and leave in the refrigerator to marinate for a few hours.

> ### TIP
> *To boost the orange flavor, add a few orange segments to the juice.*

2. Place the raisins in a microwave-safe dish and cover with the remaining sherry. Cook on *MEDIUM for 3–4 minutes*. Cover and leave to stand.

3. Cook the pork on *MEDIUM for 10 minutes* in a combination microwave preheated to 400°F (fan-assisted 350°F). Add the orange juice to the meat juices, and cook on the same settings for a further 10 minutes. Add the soaked raisins and sherry, cook on the same settings for a further 15–20 minutes until brown and crisp.

4. Remove the meat from the oven, cover with aluminum foil and leave to stand. If necessary, reduce the sauce by boiling *on HIGH for 2–3 minutes*.

5. Cut the pork into thin slices and pour the sauce over it.
This roast tastes delicious cold.

Serving suggestions: green pasta or white bread and snowpeas.

Recommended drink: a light red wine.

GROUND BEEF ROLL

SERVES 10–12 ■ ■

Combination microwave oven
Preparation and cooking time: 1 hour 10 minutes
Kcal per serving if serving 12: 470
P = 32g, F = 30g, C = 19g

2 bread rolls
2 onions
2 garlic cloves
6 ounces raw Parma ham, thinly sliced
1¼ pounds frozen puff dough
2¾ pounds mixed ground meats
1 tsp minced oregano
1 tbsp minced basil
2 eggs
3 egg yolks
salt
freshly ground black pepper
1 tbsp herb mustard
8 x baby Mozzarella cheeses (about 8 ounces)

1. Place the rolls in a bowl, cover with cold water, and set aside to soak. Peel and chop the onions, and garlic. Reserve 8 slices of the ham and chop the remainder or grind in a food processor.
2. Arrange the puff dough sheets side by side in the microwave and thaw on *LOW for 2–3 minutes.*
3. Place the meat in a bowl. Squeeze the water from the rolls. Mix together the meat, rolls, onions, garlic, chopped ham, oregano, and basil. Add the eggs and 2 egg yolks, and work to a smooth mixture. Season with salt, pepper, and mustard.
4. Dampen the dough sheets, place them next to each other, slightly overlapping, and roll to a rectangle 12 x 15 inches.
5. Shape the meat mixture into a long roll and place on the dough. Make a trough along the center of the meat roll, and line it first with ham slices and then with the Mozzarella cheeses. Wrap

Using a food processor makes a really smooth meat mixture.

the ham around the cheese, and then cover with the meat dough.
6. Wrap the dough around the meat roll, and press the edges together firmly. Beat the remaining egg yolk. Cut stars or leaves from the pastry trimmings to decorate the roll. Brush the surface with the egg yolk, place the decorations in position, and brush them with the egg yolk.
7. Place the meat roll on the lower shelf and cook on *LOW for 30–35 minutes* in a combination microwave preheated to 425°F (fan-assisted 400°F) until golden-brown.
For an even tastier meat roll, add some chopped tomatoes or peppers to the meat mixture.
Serving suggestions: fresh tomato sauce and salad. If serving the meat roll cold, remoulade sauce and a mixed salad, make an ideal accompaniment.
Recommended drink: a light red wine.

PORK CHOPS WITH MANGO SAUCE

SERVES 6 ■

Combination microwave oven
Preparation and cooking time: 30 minutes
Kcal per serving: 310
P = 23g, F = 21g, C = 7g

6 xpork chops (about 6 ounces)
salt
freshly ground black pepper
2 tbsps curry powder
2 tbsps grated root ginger
1 large ripe mango
2 tbsps vegetable oil
2 tbsps crème fraîche

1. Pat the chops dry and rub salt, pepper, half the curry powder, and half the ginger into the flesh.
2. Peel the mango and cut the flesh away from the stone.
3. Brush a microwave-safe roasting pan with half the oil and arrange the chops side by side. Cook on *LOW for 5–6 minutes* with the broiler on.
4. Meanwhile, purée the mango flesh with the crème fraîche, using a hand-held blender, and season with salt, pepper, and the remaining curry powder, and the ginger.
5. Turn the chops over and coat with the fruit purée. Cook on *LOW for a further 5–6 minutes* with the broiler on.
Serving suggestion: basmati rice.
Recommended drink: a crisp white wine.

SPARERIBS

SERVES 4 ■

Combination microwave oven
Preparation and cooking time: 40 minutes
Marinate for 1 hour
Kcal per serving: 385
P = 29g, F = 25g, C = 1g

2½ pounds pork spareribs
2 garlic cloves
2 onions
2 tbsps tomato paste
1 tbsp hot mustard
3 tbsps soy sauce
2 tbsps vegetable oil
1 tsp caraway seeds
1 tbsp sweet paprika
pinch cayenne pepper
salt
freshly ground black pepper
1 cup Guiness

1. Wash and dry the ribs and chop into 3–4-inch lengths.
2. Peel and chop the garlic and onions. Mix together the garlic, onions, tomato paste, mustard, soy sauce, and oil. Stir in the caraway seeds, paprika, and cayenne pepper, and season with salt and pepper. Brush the marinade over the pork ribs and leave for 1 hour.
3. Place the marinated ribs on a grill pan with a drip-pan. Cook on *MEDIUM for 10 minutes* in a combination microwave preheated to 425°F (fan-assisted 400°F). Turn the ribs over, brush with beer and cook on the same settings for a further 10–15 minutes until crisp and well-browned.
4. Remove the ribs, cover and keep warm. Pour the contents of the drip-pan into a pitcher. Pour off any fat. Warm through on *HIGH for 3–4 minutes.*
Serving suggestion: potato salad.
Recommended drink: beer or red wine.

LOIN OF LAMB WITH AN OLIVE CRUST

SERVES 4 ■ ■
Combination microwave oven
Preparation and cooking time: 40 minutes
Kcal per serving: 900
P = 33g, F = 81g, C = 4g

2¾ pounds loin of lamb
salt
freshly ground black pepper
10 black olives, stoned
2 garlic cloves
½ tsp minced thyme
¼ tsp minced rosemary
¼ tsp minced sage
1 tbsp French mustard
2 tbsps breadcrumbs
2–3 tbsps olive oil
½ cup dry red wine
3 tbsps chilled butter

Spread the herb paste evenly over the loin.

Dice the chilled butter and beat it into the sauce.

1. Cut two slits in the skin and fat on either side of the backbone. Rinse the lamb and pat dry. Rub salt and pepper into the flesh.
2. Chop the olives. Peel and finely chop the garlic. Mix together the olives, garlic, thyme, rosemary, sage, mustard, and breadcrumbs. Add sufficient oil to make a workable paste.
3. Place the lamb on an ovenproof, microwave-safe dish and spread with the olive-and-herb paste. Cook on *MEDIUM for 16–20 minutes* in a combination microwave preheated to 425°F (fan-assisted 400°F) until golden-brown. The cooking time depends on whether the meat is to be rare, medium or well-done. Use a meat thermometer to check the internal temperature.
4. Remove the lamb, wrap in aluminum foil, and leave to stand. Pour the wine into the meat juices and reduce on *HIGH for 4–5 minutes.* Dice the butter and beat into the sauce.

5. Detach the meat from the bone and cut into slices. Serve the sauce separately. The meat continues to cook in the foil, so it is advisable to remove it from the oven just before it has reached the required temperature.
Serving suggestions: dauphinois potatoes and broiled tomatoes.
Recommended drink: a dry rosé wine.

SHOULDER OF LAMB COOKED IN A CLAY POT

SERVES 4 ■
Standard microwave oven
Preparation and cooking time: 1 hour
Kcal per serving: 415
P = 44g, F = 20g, C = 10g

1 boneless shoulder of lamb
salt
freshly ground black pepper
3–4 garlic cloves
1 onion
2 yellow bell peppers
1 red bell pepper
1 fresh chili
4 beefsteak tomatoes
5 tbsps olive oil
1 tsp chopped fresh thyme
½ cup dry white wine
1 tbsp chopped fresh parsley

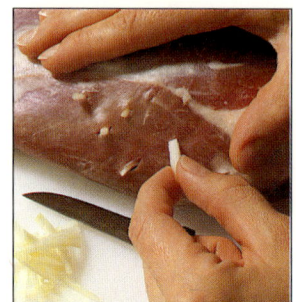

Stud the shoulder of lamb with slivers of garlic.

Cook the lamb in the microwave on a bed of vegetables.

1. Soak the clay pot in cold water.
2. Rinse the lamb and pat dry. Rub salt and pepper into the meat. Peel the garlic cloves, cut them into long slivers, and stud the meat.

TIP

Sliced potatoes may also be added to the pepper-and-tomato mixture.

3. Peel the onion and cut into matchstick strips. Halve, seed, and wash the peppers and chili and cut into strips.
4. Score the tomato skins, dip in water and cook, covered, at *HIGH for 3–4 minutes.* Rinse in cold water, skin, seed, and chop.
5. Place the vegetables in the clay pot, pour over the oil and season with thyme, salt, and pepper. Place the lamb roast on top and pour over the wine. Cover and cook on *HIGH for 20 minutes.* Turn the lamb over and cook on the same settings for a further 20–25 minutes.

6. Remove the meat, cover, and leave to stand for a few minutes. Cut into slices and serve on the vegetables. Garnish with the parsley.
Serving suggestion: white bread.
Recommended drink: a strong red wine.

Lean Cuisine

Stay slim by eating meat – for many there could scarcely be a better way of dieting. Forget those meager, unsatisfying snacks! Enjoy your food, but keep that extra weight at bay. The recipes in this section use lean cuts of beef, veal, lamb, and pork, fat is kept to a minimum, and seasoning and herbs help to keep an acceptable calorie balance. As a rule, rich breadcrumb coatings, an excess of fat for frying, and creamy sauces have been avoided; meat is boiled, braised, or broiled. If frying is essential for color or texture, then a nonstick skillet is recommended so that the need for oil and fat is limited – the ideal solution for all those who want to cut back on calories, but not on spiciness and flavor.

Beef with Radicchio and Tomatoes (recipe page 112)

BEEF OLIVES WITH VEGETABLE FILLING

SERVES 6 ■■

Preparation and cooking time: 2½ hours
Kcal per serving: 245
P = 34g, F = 6g, C = 5g

1 large carrot
½ cup green beans
2 sticks celery
1 small red pepper
salt
freshly ground white pepper
1¾ pounds beef topside, thinly sliced
7 ounces finely ground veal or veal sausagemeat
2 tbsps grated Parmesan cheese
1 garlic clove
1 tbsp minced parsley
¼ tsp minced thyme
2 sage leaves, chopped
2 tbsps olive oil
1 cup full-bodied red wine

1. Peel and dice the carrots. Trim and dice the beans and celery. Halve, seed, wash, and dice the pepper. Blanch the carrot, beans, celery, and pepper in lightly-salted boiling water for 2 minutes. Plunge them straight into ice-cold water and drain.
2. Pat the beef dry and pound with a steak hammer until the slices are half as thick but retain their shape. Rub a little salt and pepper into both sides.
3. Mix together the ground veal or sausagemeat, and Parmesan cheese. Peel and finely chop the garlic. Add the parsley, thyme, sage, and garlic to the veal or sausagemeat mixture, stir well, and season with salt and pepper.
4. Add the carrot, beans, pepper, and celery to the filling, and divide between the beef slices, spreading it evenly. Roll up from the narrow sides and secure with trussing thread.

Spread the vegetable filling onto the flattened slices of topside.

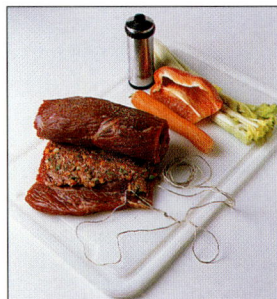
Roll up the olives and secure with trussing thread.

5. Heat the oil in a roasting pan, and fry the olives until well-browned all over. Add the wine, bring to the boil, cover and simmer for 2 hours, turning the olives occasionally. If necessary, add a little water.
6. Remove the olives from the pan, cover, and leave to stand. If required, reduce the sauce a little. Arrange the olives on a serving dish, and pour the sauce over them.
Serving suggestions: white bread and grilled tomatoes.

BOILED SIRLOIN WITH VEGETABLES

SERVES 4 ■■

Preparation and cooking time: 1½ hours
Kcal per serving: 235
P = 26g, F = 12g, C = 6g

3 carrots
½ celery head
1 onion
½ lemon
1 quart water
2 bayleaves
1 thyme sprig
1½ pounds sirloin
salt
freshly ground black pepper
1 small leek
2 tbsps butter
juice of ½ lemon
3 tbsps snipped chives

1. Peel the carrots and chop 1 of them. Trim and wash the celery and finely chop 1 stick. Peel and halve the onion. Slice the lemon. Place the chopped carrot and celery, the onion, lemon, water, bayleaves, and thyme in a flameproof casserole and bring to the boil.

TIP

The quality of the sirloin is an important factor in the success of this dish. If a good sirloin is not available, use the middle section of a beef filet. Reduce the cooking time by 20 minutes.

---

2. Rinse the sirloin and pat dry. Season with salt and pepper.
3. Season broth with salt, add the sirloin, cover, and simmer for 30 minutes. The flesh should remain pink in the middle.

Trim and peel the washed vegetables and then cut them into matchstick strips.

Cook the vegetables in the melted butter and broth until tender but still firm.

4. Meanwhile, cut the remaining carrots and celery into matchstick strips. Trim and wash the leek and cut into matchstick strips.
5. Melt the butter in a non-stick skillet, and gently fry the carrots, celery, and leek. Season with salt and pepper, and sprinkle with lemon juice. Add 1 cup of the cooking liquid from the meat. Cook the vegetables for 5–7 minutes until tender but still firm.
6. Meanwhile, remove the meat from the pan, cover, and leave to stand for a few minutes. Slice the meat thinly and arrange on a dish with the vegetables. Sprinkle with chives and serve.
Serving suggestion: boiled potatoes.

BEEF WITH RADICCHIO AND TOMATOES

(photograph page 108)

SERVES 4
Preparation and cooking time: 30 minutes
Kcal per serving: 280
P = 27g, F = 18g, C = 3g

1½ pounds beef filet
1–2 garlic cloves
salt
freshly ground black pepper
1 radicchio
1 onion
4 small beefsteak tomatoes
2 tbsps olive oil
1 tbsp lemon juice
6–8 basil leaves, chopped

1. Rinse the beef and pat dry. Cut it into ½-inch strips. Peel and crush the garlic. Season the beef with salt, pepper, and garlic.
2. Wash, trim, and shred the radicchio. Peel and chop the onion. Blanch skin, seed, and chop the tomatoes.
3. Heat the oil in a nonstick skillet, and fry the beef strips until well browned. Remove from the pan and keep warm.
4. Gently fry the onion and radicchio in the same pan over a medium heat. Add the tomatoes, sprinkle with the lemon juice, cover, and simmer for 3–4 minutes.
5. Return the meat to the pan, and warm through, stirring occasionally. Season with pepper and garnish with chopped basil leaves.
Serving suggestions: white bread.

FILET STEAKS WITH RED WINE AND ONIONS

SERVES 2
Preparation and cooking time: 30 minutes
Kcal per serving: 320
P = 38g, F = 13g, C = 3g

2 small onions
½ cup full-bodied red wine
1 tsp red wine vinegar
salt
freshly ground black pepper
2 filet steaks (about 6 ounces each)
2 tbsps vegetable oil

1. Peel and finely chop the onions. Place in a small saucepan with the wine and vinegar. Bring to the boil, and continue to boil until the liquid has evaporated. Season with salt and pepper and set aside to cool.
2. Pat the steaks dry and rub pepper into the flesh. Heat the oil in a nonstick skillet, and fry the steaks over a medium heat for 2–4 minutes on each side, depending on whether you prefer steak rare or well-done.
3. Remove the steaks, season with salt, and keep warm. Add the red wine, onions to the pan juices, warm through, and spoon onto the steaks.
Red wine, onions can also be served with roasts.
Serving suggestion: boiled potatoes and a salad.

RUSSIAN-STYLE ROUND STEAKS

SERVES 2
Preparation and cooking time: 20 minutes
Kcal per serving: 320
P = 32g, F = 21g, C = 1g

2 round steaks (about 6 ounces each)
salt
freshly ground black pepper
1 tbsp oil
1 shallot
1 pickle
1 tbsp Dijon mustard
1 tsp freshly-grated horseradish

1. Make a few cuts in the fat on each steak. Pat dry and sprinkle with pepper.
2. Heat the oil in a nonstick skillet, and fry the steaks over a high heat for 1 minute on each side. Lower the heat, and fry each side for 2–4 minutes, depending on whether you prefer steak rare or well-done.
3. Meanwhile, peel and finely chop the shallot. Finely chop the pickle. Mix together the shallot, pickle and mustard.
4. Remove the steaks from the pan, season with salt and coat with the mustard mixture and a sprinkling of grated horseradish. Serve immediately.
Serving suggestion: mashed potato and beets.

> **TIP**
>
> *Round steaks are taken from the sirloin and are about 1 inch thick; they usually have a fatty strip on one side.*

HAMBURGERS WITH BRAISED TOMATOES

SERVES 4
Preparation and cooking time: 30 minutes
Kcal per serving: 220
P = 31g, F = 9g, C = 4g

1 onion
1¼ pounds lean ground beef
½ cup quark
salt
freshly ground black pepper
1 tsp herb mustard
4 beefsteak tomatoes
1–2 garlic cloves, crushed
2 tbsps olive oil
1 tbsp minced oregano or 1 tsp dried oregano
1 tbsp minced parsley

1. Peel and finely chop the onion. Knead together the ground beef, quark, and onion to make a workable mixture. Season well with salt, pepper, and mustard, and shape into 4 large, flat burgers.
2. Blanch, skin, quarter, and seed the tomatoes. Peel and crush the garlic.
3. Heat the oil in a nonstick skillet, and fry the burgers over a medium heat for 2 minutes on each side. Arrange the tomatoes around the burgers, add the garlic, and sprinkle with oregano. Cover and simmer for 4–5 minutes.
4. Transfer the burgers to a warm serving dish. Top with the tomatoes and sprinkle with parsley.
To add a little extra flavor, top each burger with a slice of Mozzarella cheese for the last few minutes.
Serving suggestion: baked jacket potatoes.

HAMBURGERS WITH PEPPER SAUCE

SERVES 4 ■
Preparation and cooking time: 40 minutes
Kcal per serving: 385
P = 33g, F = 24g, C = 8g

4 ounces lean, raw ham
14 ounces ground beef
1 onion
1–2 garlic cloves
1 egg
1 tbsp low-fat yogurt
salt
freshly ground black pepper
1 tsp sweet paprika
pinch cayenne pepper

FOR THE PEPPER SAUCE:
1 onion
1 yellow bell pepper
1 red bell pepper
2 beefsteak tomatoes
2 tbsps vegetable oil
½ cup meat broth
salt
freshly ground black pepper
pinch sweet paprika
pinch cayenne pepper
1 tbsp chopped parsley

Grind the ham in a food processor. Mix with the other ingredients and knead.

Gently fry the onion and peppers in the meat juices, season well and then simmer in the broth.

1. Chop the ham and mix with the ground beef. Peel and chop the onion and garlic. Mix together the onion, garlic, egg, and quark, and add to the meat mixture. Knead to make a smooth mixture, and season with salt, pepper, paprika, and cayenne pepper. Shape the meat into four hamburgers.
2. To make the sauce, peel and chop the onion. Halve, seed, wash and dice the peppers. Blanch, skin, seed, and chop the tomatoes.
3. Heat the oil in a nonstick skillet, and fry the hamburgers for 3–4 minutes on each side. Remove from the pan and keep warm.
4. Stir-fry the onion and peppers in the same pan. Add the tomatoes and broth, and season with salt, pepper, paprika, and cayenne pepper. Stir thoroughly, cover and simmer for 15 minutes.

5. Place the burgers in the sauce and heat through for about 3 minutes. Serve garnished with parsley.
Serving suggestion: boiled potatoes or green tagliatelle.

MEATLOAF WITH HERBS

SERVES 4 ■
Preparation and cooking time: 1 hour 10 minutes
Kcal per serving: 415
P = 37g, F = 27g, C = 6g

1 thick slice white bread
4 slices lean raw ham
1½ pounds ground beef
1 egg
1 onion
1 large carrot
3 tbsps minced parsley
1 tsp minced marjoram
2 minced sage leaves
1 tsp minced fresh thyme
grated rind of 1 lemon
1 tsp herb mustard
salt
freshly ground black pepper
1 tbsp butter
½ cup meat broth
2 beefsteak tomatoes

Combine the ham and ground beef. Peel and shred the carrot.

Shape all the ingredients into a meatloaf. Place in a well-greased casserole.

1. Place the bread in a bowl, cover with water, and set aside to soak. Finely grind the ham in a food processor. Mix together the ham and ground beef. Squeeze out the water from the bread. Combine the bread with the meat mixture, add the egg, and stir well.
2. Peel and chop the onion. Peel and finely grate the carrot. Add the onion, carrot, 2 tbsps of the parsley, the marjoram, sage, thyme, and lemon rind to the meat mixture. Knead thoroughly to form a smooth mixture, and season with mustard, salt, and pepper. Shape into a long meatloaf.
3. Grease an oval casserole with half the butter, and dice the remaining butter. Place the meatloaf in the casserole and dot with butter. Bake in a preheated oven at 400°F for 15 minutes. Add the broth, and return to the oven for a further 15–25 minutes.
4. Blanch, skin, seed, and chop the tomatoes.
5. Remove the meatloaf

from the casserole. Add the tomatoes to the casserole and warm through over a medium heat. Stir in the remaining parsley.
6. Cut the meatloaf into slices and arrange on a warm serving dish. Hand the sauce separately.
This meatloaf also tastes delicious cold.
Serving suggestion: mashed potato, and Brussels sprouts or a mixed salad.

HUNGARIAN VEAL GOULASH

SERVES 4 ■

*Preparation and cooking
time: 1 hour
Kcal per serving: 235
P = 27g, F = 11g, C = 6g*

2 small red peppers
4 onions
2 slices lean raw ham
2 tbsps vegetable oil
14 ounces boneless veal,
    cubed
salt
freshly ground black pepper
1 tbsp sweet paprika
1 tsp chopped fresh
    marjoram
2 cups meat broth
2 tbsps sour cream
1 tbsp minced parsley

1. Halve, seed, wash, and chop the peppers. Peel and chop the onions. Chop the ham.
2. Heat the oil in a flame-proof casserole, and fry the onions, peppers, and ham for 5 minutes over a medium heat.
3. Add the veal, and season with salt, pepper, paprika, and marjoram. Mix thoroughly and fry for a further 5 minutes, stirring occasionally. Add the broth, cover and simmer for 30 minutes.
4. Stir in the sour cream, heat through, and garnish the goulash with parsley.
Serving suggestions: boiled potatoes or noodles and a green salad.

TIP

The addition of a diced potato will give the goulash sauce a thicker, floury consistency.

ROAST VEAL WITH ROSEMARY

SERVES 4 ■

*Preparation and cooking
time: 2 hours
Kcal per serving: 235
P = 30g, F = 9g, C = 5g*

1¼ pounds topside of veal
2 garlic cloves
salt
freshly ground black pepper
2 sprigs fresh rosemary
2 thin slices Parma ham
1 onion
2 sticks celery
4 beefsteak tomatoes
1 tbsp olive oil
½ cup dry white wine
2 tbsps minced parsley

1. Wash the veal and pat dry. Peel and crush the garlic. Rub the veal with salt, pepper, and garlic. Lay the rosemary on the joint and cover with overlapping slices of ham. Secure them with trussing thread.
2. Peel and dice the onion. Trim, wash, and dice the celery. Blanch, skin, seed, and chop the tomatoes.
3. Heat the oil in a roasting pan, and fry the meat until browned all over. Add the onion and celery, and gently fry for a further 5 minutes. Add the tomatoes and wine, and bring to the boil.
4. Cover and cook in a preheated oven at 400°F for 45 minutes. Baste the meat with the cooking juices from time to time. Remove the lid and continue to cook for a further 15 minutes.
5. Remove the meat, wrap in aluminum foil, and leave to stand for a few minutes. Warm the sauce over a low heat, and stir in the parsley.
6. Cut the veal into slices and arrange on a warm serving platter. Hand the sauce separately.

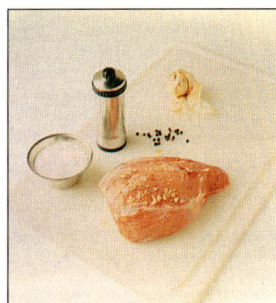

Rub salt, pepper and garlic into the veal.

Arrange the rosemary sprigs on the meat.

Wrap slices of ham around the meat and secure them with trussing thread.

Serving suggestions: penne or potato gnocchi and a mixed salad.

FILET OF VEAL WITH CARAMELIZED ONIONS

SERVES 2 ■

*Preparation and cooking
time: 30 minutes
Kcal per serving: 295
P = 32g, F = 7g, C = 13g*

6 onions
1 tbsp vegetable oil
1 tsp sugar
10 ounces filet of veal
salt
freshly ground white pepper
½ cup rosé wine

1. Peel and quarter the onions. Heat the oil in a nonstick skillet, and gently fry the onions over a medium heat for a few minutes.
2. Sprinkle sugar over the onions and stir well. Cook until the sugar begins to caramelize.
3. Rinse the veal and pat dry. Rub salt and pepper into the flesh.
4. Push the onions to the edge of the skillet, add the veal, and fry until browned all over.
5. Add the wine, cover, and cook for 6–8 minutes, stirring occasionally.
Serving suggestion: crusty white bread.

VEAL OLIVES WITH SAUSAGEMEAT FILLING

SERVES 4 ■
Preparation and cooking time: 1 hour 10 minutes
Kcal per serving: 310
P = 44g, F = 8g, C = 9g

½ cup fresh, shelled peas
salt
freshly ground white pepper
6 ounces veal sausagemeat
2 tbsps Low-fat cottage cheese
2 tbsps minced mixed herbs
pinch grated nutmeg
grated rind of ½ lemon
4 long, thin veal scallops
   (about 6 ounces each)
1 small onion
1 carrot
1 stick celery
1 tbsp oil
1 tbsp butter
½ cup dry white wine
½ cup veal stock

1. Blanch the peas in lightly salted boiling water, plunge in ice-cold water, and set aside to drain.
2. Mix together the sausage-meat and cottage cheese. Stir in the herbs and peas, and season with nutmeg, lemon rind, salt, and pepper.

TIP

Instead of veal sausagemeat, try pork sausagemeat. The filling will be tastier although higher in calories.

---

3. Pat the veal dry, and flatten carefully with a steak hammer. Rub salt and pepper into the meat, and coat each scallop with a layer of the sausagemeat mixture. Roll up the scallops, starting from the long side, and secure with cocktail sticks.

Roll up the scallops, starting from the long side, and secure with cocktail sticks or trussing thread.

Fry the olives with the chopped vegetables. Add the wine and broth, and cook for 30 minutes.

4. Peel and chop the onion and carrot. Trim, wash, and chop the celery.
5. Heat the oil and butter in a flameproof casserole, and fry the veal olives until browned all over. Add the onion, carrot, and celery, and fry for a further 5 minutes. Pour in the wine and broth, cover and simmer for 30 minutes.
6. Remove the olives from the casserole and keep warm. Rub the sauce through a sieve, return to the casserole, and allow to reduce a little over a high heat. Pour over the veal olives and serve.
Serving suggestions: green tagliatelle and carrots.

ROMAN-STYLE VEAL OLIVES

SERVES 4 ■
Preparation and cooking time: 20 minutes
Kcal per serving: 290
P = 32g, F = 16g, C = 2g

8 veal scallops (about 4
   ounces each)
salt
freshly ground black pepper
2 slices Parma ham
1 tsp minced sage
2 tbsps oil
4 tbsps Marsala
4 tbsps veal broth
1 tbsp chilled butter

1. Pat the scallops dry, and flatten carefully with a steak hammer. Season with salt and pepper.
2. Chop the ham, and mix with the sage. Divide the ham mixture between the scallops. Roll up the scallops, starting from the long side, and secure the ends with cocktail sticks.
3. Heat the oil in a nonstick skillet, and fry the olives until browned all over. Add the Marsala and broth. Cover and cook for 2–3 minutes.
4. Remove the olives from the pan and keep warm. Bring the sauce to the boil over a high heat and allow to reduce slightly.
5. Dice the butter, and beat into the sauce, a few pieces at a time. Pour the sauce over the olives and serve.
Serving suggestions: white bread and garden peas.

VEAL CUTLETS WITH GREEN ONIONS

SERVES 2 ■
Preparation and cooking time: 25 minutes
Kcal per serving: 270
P = 33g, F = 10g, C = 3g

2 veal cutlets (about 8
   ounces each)
1 garlic clove
½ tsp dried thyme
salt
freshly ground white pepper
bunch of small green onions
   (scallions)
1 tbsp oil
½ cup white wine
1 tbsp white wine vinegar

1. Pat the cutlets dry. Peel and crush the garlic. Rub the cutlets with the garlic, thyme, salt, and pepper.
2. Trim, wash and chop the green onions.
3. Heat the oil in a nonstick skillet, and fry the cutlets over a medium heat for 2 minutes on each side. Remove the meat, and fry the green onions in the same pan. Add the wine and vinegar, return the cutlets to the pan, cover, and cook for 8–10 minutes.
4. Arrange the veal on warmed plates and top with the green onions. If necessary, reduce the sauce a little and then pour it over the onions.
Serving suggestion: white bread.

TIP

Try cooking lamb with green onions in this way.

SWEET-AND-SOUR PORK

SERVES 4 ▪
*Preparation and cooking
time: 40 minutes
Kcal per serving: 395
P = 20g, F = 24g, C = 14g*

14 ounces pork filet
1 tsp cornstarch
2 tbsps soy sauce
1 tbsp sherry vinegar
6 tbsps rice wine or dry
    sherry
1 tsp tomato paste
1 tsp freshly grated
    horseradish
pinch cayenne pepper
½ pineapple
1 small leek
1 small red bell pepper
1 small yellow bell pepper
1 chili
3 tbsps groundnut oil
salt
freshly ground black pepper

1. Rinse the pork and pat
dry. Trim, if necessary, and
cut into slices.
2. Mix together the cornstarch, soy sauce, vinegar,
rice wine, or sherry, tomato
paste, and horseradish in a
shallow dish. Season the
pork with cayenne pepper
and place in the marinade.
Set aside for 15 minutes.

┌─────── **TIP** ───────┐

*This is a low-
calorie but still
very tasty
variation of a
traditional
Chinese recipe, in
which the meat is
first dipped in
coating, then
fried in hot oil,
and finally
dipped in a
vegetable sauce.*

└──────────────────┘

3. Meanwhile, peel, core,
and dice the pineapple.
Trim, wash, and slice the

*Mix the meat, pineapple, and the
reserved marinade with the fried
vegetables and warm through.*

leek. Halve, seed, wash, and
dice the peppers. Halve,
seed, wash, and finely chop
the chili.
4. Heat 2 tbsps of the oil in a
wok or skillet, and stir-fry the
leek, peppers, and chili over
a medium heat for 5–6 minutes.
5. Heat the remaining oil in a
nonstick skillet. Drain the
pork and reserve the marinade. Fry the pork over a
high heat until browned on
both sides.
6. Mix the meat, pineapple
and the reserved marinade
with the fried vegetables and
heat through over a high
heat for 2–3 minutes.
7. Season with salt and pepper and serve immediately.
Serving suggestion: fluffy
boiled rice.

PORK WITH CHINESE CABBAGE

SERVES 2 ▪
*Preparation and cooking
time: 30 minutes
Kcal per serving: 325
P = 24g, F = 25g, C = 1g*

1 head Chinese (Nappa)
    cabbage
8 ounces pork filet
2 tbsps sesame oil
salt
freshly ground white pepper
1 tsp grated root ginger
1 tsp mild curry powder
2 tbsps soy sauce
1 tsp minced coriander
    (cilantro) leaves

1. Discard any wilted outer
leaves from the Chinese
cabbage and cut it in half.
Remove the tough stalk and
shred the leaves.
2. Rinse the pork and pat
dry. Trim, if necessary, and
slice thinly.
3. Heat the oil in a wok or
skillet. Stir-fry the cabbage
for 3–5 minutes. Add the
pork, and stir-fry until
browned all over.
4. Season with salt and pepper, and add the ginger,
curry powder, and soy
sauce. Sprinkle with the
chopped coriander and
serve immediately.
If Chinese cabbage is not
available, use white cab-
bage.
Serving suggestion: fluffy,
boiled rice.

MEAT AND VEGETABLE KEBOBS

SERVES 4 ▪
*Preparation and cooking
time: 40 minutes
Marinate for 2 hours
Kcal per serving: 285
P = 21g, F = 17g, C = 5g*

14 ounces pork filet
2 small zucchini
1 red bell pepper
1 yellow bell pepper
2 onions

FOR THE MARINADE:
2 tbsps vegetable oil
2 tbsps soy sauce
3 tbsps dry sherry
1 tbsp tomato paste
pinch grated root ginger
½ tsp five-spice powder
freshly ground black pepper

1. Rinse the pork and pat
dry. Rinse, trim, and cut the
courgettes into ½-inch slices.
Halve, seed, and wash the
peppers. Cut into 1-inch
squares. Peel and quarter
the onions. Thread alternate
cubes of meat and vegeta-
bles on to 4 kebob skewers.
2. Thoroughly mix together
all the ingredients for the
marinade. Brush the mari-
nade over the kebobs, cover
and set aside for 2 hours.
3. Place the kebobs under a
preheated broiler or on a
barbecue, and cook for 5–7
minutes. Brush the kebobs
frequently with the remaining marinade.
Serving suggestion: potatoes baked in foil.

┌─────── **TIP** ───────┐

*Place a sheet of
aluminum foil
under the broiler
pan.*

└──────────────────┘

LAMB RAGOÛT WITH ARTICHOKES AND LEMON SAUCE

SERVES 4 ■■
Preparation and cooking time: 45 minutes
Kcal per serving: 475
P = 31g, F = 31g, C = 18g

8 small, young globe
   artichokes
juice of 1 lemon
1½ pounds boneless leg of
   lamb
salt
freshly ground black pepper
2 shallots
1 garlic clove
2 tbsps vegetable oil
½ cup veal broth

FOR THE LEMON SAUCE:
2 eggs, separated
salt
juice of 1 lemon
1 tbsp minced parsley

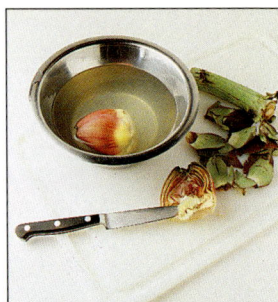
Cut off the lower artichoke leaves and the tips of the upper leaves. Halve and remove the chokes.

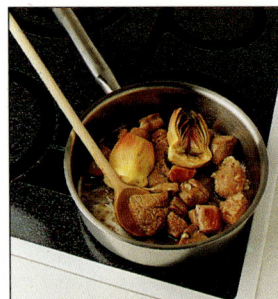
Fry the meat and artichokes, add the broth and simmer for 30 minutes.

Fold the whisked egg white mixture into the ragoût and warm through.

1. Break off the artichoke stalks and brush with lemon juice to prevent discoloration. Cut off the lower leaves and tips of the upper leaves. Halve the artichokes, discard the chokes, and place the halves in a bowl of water with the remaining lemon juice.
2. Rinse the lamb and pat dry. Cut into 1-inch cubes, and season with salt and pepper.
3. Peel and chop the shallots and garlic. Heat the oil, and fry the shallots and garlic until transparent.
4. Add the lamb and artichokes, and fry for 5 minutes, stirring frequently. Add in the broth, cover, and simmer for about 30 minutes.
5. To make the lemon sauce, whisk the egg whites with a pinch of salt until they form stiff peaks. Slowly add the lemon juice, egg yolks, and parsley. Fold the mixture into the stew, warm through quickly but do not allow to boil. As an alternative, use veal instead of lamb.
Serving suggestion: boiled potatoes or fettuccini.

BOILED SHOULDER OF LAMB ON A BED OF VEGETABLES

SERVES 4 ■
Preparation and cooking time: 1 hour 40 minutes
Kcal per serving: 630
P = 48g, F = 45g, C = 8g

2½ pounds boneless shoulder
   of lamb
2 garlic cloves
salt
freshly ground black pepper
1 onion
5 peppercorns
2 bayleaves
2 thyme sprigs
1 rosemary sprig
2 sage leaves
1 bunch mixed herbs
1 quart water
2 tbsps white wine vinegar
4 carrots
1 kohlrabi
1 cup tender green beans
1 tbsp minced parsley

Peel and crush the garlic.

Wash the sage and combine with the other herbs.

1. Rinse the lamb and pat dry. Peel and crush the garlic. Rub salt, pepper, and garlic into the meat.

> **TIP**
>
> *The smaller and succulent fore-knuckles can be cooked in this way. The choice of vegetables may vary according to the season.*

2. Peel and quarter the onion. Place the onion, peppercorns, bayleaves, thyme, rosemary, sage, and mixed herbs in a flameproof casserole. Add the water and vinegar and bring to the boil. Add the lamb, cover, and simmer for 1¼ hours.
3. Meanwhile, peel and slice the carrots. Peel the kohlrabi and cut into matchstick strips. Trim the green beans and, if necessary, remove any strings.
4. Remove the cooked lamb from the liquid, wrap in aluminum foil, and leave to stand.
5. Rub the cooking liquid through a sieve, return to the casserole, and bring to the boil. Add the carrots and kohlrabi, and cook for about 5 minutes. Add the beans, and cook until tender but still firm. Remove the vegetables with a slotted spoon and place them in a deep serving dish. Bring the cooking liquid back to the boil and allow to reduce slightly.
6. Cut the lamb into thin slices and arrange them on the vegetables. Pour over the sauce and garnish with chopped parsley.
Serving suggestion: boiled potatoes.

Index